TEC

SERIES EDITOR: LEE JOHNSON

W9-CSX-158

OSPREY MILITARY ELITE SERIES: 67

PIRATES
1660-1730

TEXT BY
ANGUS KONSTAM

COLOUR PLATES BY
ANGUS MCBRIDE

First published in Great Britain in 1998 by Osprey Publishing
Elms Court, Chapel Way, Botley, Oxford OX2 9LP United Kingdom

© 1998 Osprey Publishing Limited

All rights reserved. Apart from any fair dealing for the purpose of private study, research, criticism or review, as permitted under the Copyright, Designs and Patents Act, 1988, no part of this publication may be reproduced, stored in a retrieval system, or transmitted in any form or by any means, electronic, electrical, chemical, mechanical, optical, photocopying, recording or otherwise, without the prior permission of the copyright owner. Enquiries should be addressed to the Publishers.

ELITE 67: PIRATES 1660–1730   ISBN 1 85532 706 6
PIRATES!   ISBN 1 85532 837 2

Filmset in Great Britain
Printed through World Print Ltd., Hong Kong

98 99 00 01 02   10 9 8 7 6 5 4 3 2 1

Editors: Sharon van der Merwe and Marcus Cowper
Design: Gwyn Lewis

FOR A CATALOGUE OF ALL BOOKS PUBLISHED BY OSPREY MILITARY PLEASE WRITE TO:
The Marketing Manager, Osprey Publishing Ltd., P.O. Box 140, Wellingborough
Northants NN8 4ZA United Kingdom

Acknowledgements

My special thanks to Dr. Madeleine Burnside and Dylan Kibler (Mel Fisher Maritime Museum), David D. Moore (North Carolina Maritime Museum, and the excavator of Blackbeard's ship), and the inhabitants of Key West (the last true pirate den).

Artist's Note

Readers may care to note that the original paintings from which the colour plates in this book were prepared are available for private sale. All reproduction copyright whatsoever is retained by the Publisher. All enquiries should be addressed to:

Scorpio, P.O. Box 475, Hailsham, E. Sussex BN27 2SL UK

The publishers regret that they can enter into no correspondence upon this matter.

TITLE PAGE **The pirate Stede Bonnet, shown wearing a wig and armed with a musket. The engraver has incorrectly shown the flag of the pirate Richard Worley instead of Bonnet's. Worley was a small-time pirate killed off Charleston in 1718.**

PIRATES

INTRODUCTION

The pirate Edward Low in a hurricane, with a three-masted ship foundering in the background. Low was active in the Caribbean from December 1721 until he was marooned by his own crew in early 1724. A sadistic captain, he frequently tortured and mutilated captives before killing them. He even was accused of cutting off captives' ears, lips or hearts and making other prisoners eat them.

When we think of pirates, we usually imagine those who operated in the Caribbean and the American eastern seaboard during the decade on each side of 1700. In fact, pirates were around for a lot longer than that. Julius Caesar was captured by pirates before Pompey swept them from the Roman *Mare Nostrum* (the Mediterranean). Pirates plagued medieval and Renaissance shipping from the Baltic to the Mediterranean, and Barbary Coast pirates operated until well into the 19th century. As European explorers ventured further afield they encountered new forms of piracy, off Africa, in the Indian Ocean and in the Pacific. Rivalry between European powers as they carved out overseas empires also provided the nucleus for a resurgence of piracy in foreign waters, often sponsored by European powers. These 'privateers' were pirates in all but name, and their ranks included national heroes, such as Drake, Hawkins and Frobisher. As the spread of Spanish rivals into the Caribbean continued in the 17th century, a more organised form of piracy began. Buccaneer fleets plagued Spanish shipping, coastal towns, and later major cities. Although not strictly pirates, their actions were piratical in nature, but often carried the blessing of their sovereign country. The end of the buccaneer era in the late 17th century gave rise to the period known as 'the golden age of piracy', which encompassed piratical actions in the Americas as well as in the Indian Ocean and the South China seas. Although the 'golden age' ended around 1730, piracy continued to be practised by non-Europeans in the Far East. The police actions of European powers did much to stamp out piratical activity during the subsequent centuries, but piracy is still alive and well today. Indonesian waters are still plagued by modern-day pirates, equipped with fast speedboats and assault rifles. Although the methods have changed, the basic nature of violent crime and extortion on the high seas is the same as it was in the time of Caesar.

Hollywood and the writers of historical fiction have done much to glamorise piracy, particularly piracy during 'the golden age'. Characters such as Blackbeard, Captain Kidd and Black Bart have become the stuff of legend.

Edward England, a pirate who operated first in the Caribbean, then the Indian Ocean between 1717 and 1719. The mercy he customarily showed to captives led to his crew removing him as captain and putting him ashore on Mauritius. He reputedly ended his days as a beggar in Madagascar.

The aim of this book is to strip away the glamour and myth, allowing the true nature of piracy to be revealed. Instead of a life of romantic glamour, with crews led by aristocratic swashbuckling heroes, the average pirate was a doomed man, lacking the education, abilities and pragmatism to escape his inevitable fate. A pirate's life was usually nasty, brutish and short.

Words such as 'buccaneer', 'pirate' and 'swashbuckler' have frequently been bandied about, and are often used indiscriminately. Before we continue we should define them more clearly.

A *buccaneer* was the name given to backwoodsmen on modern Haiti in the mid-17th century. It later came to be used when speaking of the mainly English and French raiders of the Spanish Main, who acted as semi-legalised pirates, based in Port Royal and Tortuga. A *freebooter* or *filibuster* was the name given exclusively to French buccaneers, and came from the small '*flibotes*' (fly boats) they sometimes used. A *privateer* was a man or a ship under contract to a government, allowing it to attack enemy ships during wartime. This contract, called a 'Letter of Marque', meant that the government got a share of the profits. A *pirate* attacked any ship, regardless of nationality.

Sometimes the names become a little mixed up. A privateer might turn to piracy (like Captain Kidd), after a major war. Buccaneers such as Henry Morgan were really privateers, but when he attacked Panama in 1671, England and Spain were at peace, and Morgan was acting as a pirate! A swashbuckler is a Hollywood epithet, but one based on historical roots, being derived from 'sword and buckler', a preferred Spanish weapon combination in the 16th century, when 'swashbuckler' referred to a weapon-armed thug or brigand, the name coming from the sound of a sword striking a buckler. Although the word fell into disuse, it was revived by 19th century pirate fiction writers, and has remained closely linked with piracy ever since. During the 17th and 18th centuries it was never used in conjunction with piracy or piratical activities.

The Golden Age of Piracy and Sources

The end of the 17th century saw the greatest outburst of piracy in the history of seafaring. Ironically called 'the golden age of piracy', the era lasted 30 years, from around 1700 until 1730. Although the most troubled area was the Caribbean, piracy was also rife off the Eastern seaboard of America, in the Indian Ocean and off the West Coast of Africa (where the 'Pirate Round' followed the trade routes from India to America via Africa). The piracy boom was the result of circumstances: the end of a long war between Britain and France meant that ports were full of unemployed sailors and there was a lack of legal employment. The majority of the pirates who have gripped the popular imagination operated during this period, and the rise and fall of their careers form the backbone of this book. It is also important to examine these pirates against the backdrop of the ships, trade and politics affecting their world, mainly that of the American colonies and the islands of the Caribbean.

Legends in their own time, pirates such as Blackbeard and Bartholomew Roberts now seem larger than life. What we really know of them is surprisingly little, and is drawn from the recollections of ex-pirates, former victims, naval officers who encountered them, or the records of courtrooms and confessions. One other source is the book *A General History of the Robberies and Murders of the most notorious Pyrates* (1724). The author, alleged to be a Captain Charles Johnson, had extensive first-hand knowledge of piracy, and it is suggested by literary critics that Johnson

A pirate (meant to depict William Phillips, active off New England in 1722-4) is shown forcing a captive to drink a glass of rum at pistol point. The scene reflects the numerous accounts of pirates humiliating and torturing their victims for their own amusement.

was the nom-de-plume for Daniel Defoe, the author of *Robinson Crusoe*. The book concentrated on pirates operating in the 30 years before its publication. Characters such as Edward Teach ('Blackbeard'), Edward Low and Henry Every were portrayed as ogres, and their actual deeds embellished with bloodcurdling fictional anecdotes. One of the problems is that the line between fact and fiction is extremely blurred. While many elements of his portrayals were based on fact, it is vital to sift through his descriptions, comparing his version with the pirates mentioned in other contemporary accounts.

Lack of strong government in the majority of the American colonies made the seaboard a pirate hunting ground. The benefits of illicit trade between pirates and townspeople were balanced against the disruption of shipping and rising insurance prices. One by one the colonial governors clamped down on piracy in their waters, and judicial pressure was backed by naval force to put an end to the outbreak. By 1730 the era of rampant piracy was all but over. Although later outbreaks of piracy occurred, this short era would remain lodged in popular and romantic culture as the 'golden age of piracy'. The romantic-sounding name belied the cruelty, harshness and misery created by pirates, and unlike other 'golden ages' it was never regarded with any form of nostalgia. The phrase itself was never used by those who lived through it, but was subsequently applied by writers seeking to embellish the pirate story with an aura it didn't deserve.

THE PIRATE CREW

Composition

The largest source of information on the composition of pirate crews comes from court records, although one survey of seamen, and a number of personal memoirs and letters also provide valuable information. A study of 700 men indicted for piracy during the early 17th century reveals that almost three-quarters were seamen. Another analysis of early 18th century pirates shows the overwhelming majority had previously served on board merchant vessels, warships or privateers. They were therefore almost always experienced seamen and came from a variety of seafaring nations, although the majority were either English or from the American colonies. The historian David Cordingly published a study indicating that of the known pirates active in the Caribbean between 1715 and 1725, 35 per cent were English, 25 per cent colonial Americans, 20 per cent from the West Indian colonies (mainly Jamaica and Barbados), ten per cent were Scottish and eight per cent were Welsh. The remaining two per cent were from other seafaring countries, such as Sweden, Holland, France or Spain. As seamen, the majority came from port cities, such as London, Bristol, Leith, Swansea and the West Country in the British Isles, or Boston, New York or Charleston in the American colonies. The majority of seamen in the early 18th century were young men in their twenties, with an average age for seaman and pirate alike of 27. The stamina, fitness and agility required to work a sailing ship precluded many older men from crewing a vessel.

A large percentage of pirate crews were also black men, of African descent. An account of the crew of Bartholomew Roberts in 1721 reported

Daniel Defoe, the author of *Robinson Crusoe*, was a businessman turned writer who confessed a fascination with piracy. The 'Captain Charles Johnson' who wrote *A General History of the Robberies and Murders of the most notorious Pyrates* is most likely a pen-name for Defoe himself. The work has been reprinted hundreds of times since its first publication in 1724.

A sailor captures a giant turtle by turning it onto its back, from an engraving of 1724. Turtles were a popular source of meat in the Caribbean during the 18th century, and could be kept alive on board ship until required.

that they were composed of 180 white men and 48 'French Creole' black men. When his crew were captured by the Royal Navy off West Africa, the prisoners comprised 187 white and 75 black men. Many of these black men were escaped slaves from the West Indies plantations, although a number were volunteers from captured slave ships. As the racial composition contradicts that encountered in merchant or naval ships of the early 18th century, it has to be assumed that the majority of these black men were 'landsmen'. This begs the question of what exactly was their role on board a ship crewed by professional seamen. While a number of historians argue that they served on an equal footing with white men, there is a large body of evidence to suggest that they were regarded as servants, used to carry out heavy or menial tasks on board the pirate vessel. As familiarity and experience grew, these black men may have enjoyed a more integrated relationship with the crew. According to trial transcripts, a number of integrated crews existed, where Africans were considered full crew members. These men had the most to lose by capture, knowing that if they were not hanged they would be enslaved. A number of Africans, including escaped plantation slaves as well as new arrivals, did succeed in becoming pirates in their own right. One exaggerated Jamaican newspaper article of 1725 reported bands of African and African American pirates marauding the Caribbean and eating the hearts of the white men they captured.

In this William Hogarth engraving of the mid-18th century, 'the idle apprentice' is being sent to sea, where the sailors in the boat taunt him about what awaits him. One holds up a mock whip, while the other points out a hanged pirate on the shore. His mother weeps for her son.

Motivation

The majority became pirates when their merchant vessels were captured, and they elected to join the pirate crew. While landsmen would be killed or put ashore, seamen often had no choice but to sign a charter and join the crew. Many of the more successful pirates started their piratical careers in this manner. Another common route was for privateering crews to turn to piracy. The profits of war encouraged men to become privateers, and subsequently, when peace returned, this caused massive unemployment

William Hogarth's 'Gin Lane' depicts the extreme squalor found in the lower levels of 18th century English society. It also shows the hopeless plight of the poor, which forced many to become sailors, and to consider piracy as a means of improving their lot in life.

among the maritime communities of Europe, the Caribbean or the Americas. Although execution was the expected punishment and life expectancy was short, piracy was an attractive alternative to dying of starvation or becoming a beggar or thief on land.

The attraction of a pirate's life was financial; the benefit of all that hard work went to the men themselves. A seaman's life was gruelling, and often involved an existence of constant dampness and discomfort, poor conditions and ever-present danger. Drinking water was usually foul and food was often rotten and insufficient. Half of all sailors' deaths were caused by disease, ranging from scurvy to typhus, tuberculosis, dysentery and smallpox. New ports meant exposure to fresh diseases and ships were the perfect incubators for illness, with men sleeping and working in close quarters. Unlike sailors on naval or merchant vessels, pirates and privateers at least had the promise of huge financial rewards to make up for all the hardship.

Dress

Pirates were seamen, and their appearance was the same as that of other seamen of the early 18th century. While 'landsmen' of the period wore knee breeches, stockings, sleeved or sleeveless waistcoats and long coats, seamen wore their own distinctive attire. Short jackets ('fearnoughts') were popular, often cut from a heavy blue or grey cloth, and in bad weather heavier canvas coats were sometimes worn. Some illustrations show sailors of the period wearing a form of waistcoat (red or blue), either sleeved or sleeveless. Shirts were either plain linen or checked, frequently in blue and white. Knee breeches were replaced by canvas trousers or 'petticoat breeches', cut a few inches above the ankle, resembling the culottes of the French Revolution. These were reportedly cut from a 'heavy, rough red nap'. Both forms of trousers were sometimes coated in a thin lair of tar as protection against water. Shoes were often discarded altogether on board ship, although a pair would be reserved for visits ashore. If stockings were worn, grey wool was the usual form for seamen of the day. A neck scarf was commonly worn, reflecting a style common with labourers on land during the early 18th century. Headgear consisted of either a knotted scarf, a tricorne hat, a woollen 'Monmouth' cap, or a form of foul weather hat, resembling a 17th century 'montero' cap. Headgear was of vital importance as protection against the sun in the Caribbean or off the African or Indian coasts.

As well as plundering the cargo of a captured vessel, pirates would also take clothing, retaining what suited them either to wear at sea or as a suit of shore-going finery. There are records of pirates facing execution wearing velvet jackets, breeches of taffeta, silk shirts and stockings, and fine felt tricornes. These were probably taken from captives or made from plundered materials. Even in the austere navy of the time, sailors retained well-kept clothes to wear when in port. It appears from several accounts that many pirates also wore their finery when they were at sea.

Pirate captains frequently adopted the dress worn by successful merchants, giving the wearer the appearance of a gentleman. This meant wearing breeches, a waistcoat and a long outer coat. Both contemporary accounts and later illustrations support the evidence for the adoption of this gentlemanly persona. One pirate captain based on Madagascar was described in 1716 as 'dressed in a short coat, with broad plate buttons, and other things agreeable, but without shoes or stockings'. The leader in piratical elegance was Bartholomew Roberts, who, according to Johnson and contemporary accounts by his crew, 'dressed in a rich crimson damask waistcoat and breeches, a red feather in his hat, a gold chain round his neck, with a diamond cross hanging to it'.

PIRATE WARFARE

A successful pirate attack began with finding the quarry, and then attacking it. A typical pirate sloop with a look-out at the masthead could expect to see a sailing vessel up to 20 miles away, if the conditions were right. Unlike a naval

A late 17th century gun and carriage, together with its associated tools and equipment, from John Seller: *The Sea Gunner* (1692). The gunner is shown touching off the piece using a hand-held linstock and burning slowmatch. The basic elevating system of quoin and stool-bed are clearly shown.

squadron, which could string ships out in a line and thereby search a large swathe of ocean, pirate vessels often operated alone. On the rare occasions when secondary pirate vessels or prize vessels were available, they could be pressed into service to help in the search. At night, or in poor weather conditions, finding another ship was well nigh impossible. Pirates also needed to be able to identify a vessel as quickly as possible once they found it. Warships were to be avoided - in the worst cases they might be part of a larger force located over the horizon, sweeping for enemy ships or pirates.

Pirates usually operated in cruising grounds which lay across major shipping routes. The waters of the Bahamas were popular as they lay close to the narrow Florida straits, and the Bahamian shoals provided a good refuge if pursued. The Windward Channel between Cuba and Hispaniola was another popular cruising area, as were the waters off Madagascar, the West African coast and the seaboard of the American colonies. Pirates often followed seasonal patterns, preferring the Caribbean in winter and the Atlantic seaboard in summer.

Once sighted, the potential armament and crew numbers of the quarry needed to be accurately estimated, along with vessel's speed, sailing abilities and the quality of her captain. These factors were vital in determining whether the vessel could be overhauled without requiring a long chase. Once sighted and evaluated, the quarry had to be overhauled. This is why the majority of pirate crews preferred small, fast vessels such as sloops and schooners, which often had the edge over a quarry in terms of speed. In order to close within gun range, the pirate vessel also sometimes employed trickery. The use of false flags was fairly common, the hunter trying to lull the hunted into a false sense of security. Another pirate trick was to disguise a vessel by covering the gunports with a painted canvas screen, or to add impedimenta, like chicken coops, deck cargo or even female passengers in order to get close enough to attack. Similarly, many merchant vessels painted fake gunports on their sides to make their vessels look like warships and to scare the pirates off.

Once within range, the pirate vessel would usually haul down any false colours, haul up her own, and demand that the quarry surrender by firing a gun. At closer range, this would be accompanied by demands yelled between the ships with the aid of a speaking trumpet. It was well known that any form of resistance could lead to a wholesale slaughter once the pirates captured the defending ship. This meant that intimidation was a major weapon in the pirate arsenal. A

Howell Davis, a Welsh pirate who preyed on shipping off the West African coast and in the Caribbean from July 1718 until June 1719. An expert in deception, Davis was killed in a skirmish with Portuguese troops on the West African coast.

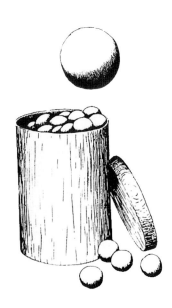

A selection of the ammunition used on board pirate vessels of the early 18th century. A basic cast-iron roundshot is accompanied by a bar-shot (to cut rigging), a canister shot of musket balls or scrap iron (anti-personnel), and a bound sabot carrying grapeshot (also designed as an anti-personnel round).

victim was then often asked to lower her boats and ferry over a pirate prize crew. A typical assault was recounted by the captain of the merchant ship *Samuel*, attacked by Bartholomew Roberts in 1721. The *Samuel* was over-hauled by two ships off the Newfoundland Banks. The larger vessel was a three-masted ship and was armed with 26 guns. There were about 100 men on board each of the vessels, and only 10 on the *Samuel*. Once overhauled, the *Samuel's* captain was ordered to lower a boat and come on board. The pirates then boarded the *Samuel*, took part of her cargo, threw the rest over-board, took the ship's boat and two guns, and press-ganged most of the crew. They were debating whether to burn the prize or not when another sail was spotted, and the pirates gave chase, leaving the *Samuel's* captain and one crewman to sail the ship back to Boston. This was typical of the majority of pirate attacks, where no resistance was offered.

If the quarry tried to defend itself, the pirates were forced to decide how best to overcome the defending vessel. Obviously, the pirates would prefer to capture a victim by boarding rather than by gunfire, which could damage their potential prize. Also, intimidation was a double-edged weapon, as fear of reprisals when captured would increase the ferocity of the defence. The mechanics of attack by gunfire or boarding were straight-forward, although effectiveness greatly depended on skill, experience and (at least for the pirates) sobriety.

Attack using gunfire

In the early 18th century, even the smallest merchant vessel carried artillery pieces (guns). To be correct, a cannon referred only to a specific size and type of ordnance. By the late 17th century, cast-iron had replaced bronze as the most common material used to manufacture ordnance, making guns cheaper and easier to produce than before. The wars of the late 17th and early 18th centuries meant that arming a vessel was a necessity. It also meant that most sailors were proficient to some extent in operating guns at sea.

A four-wheeled truck carriage was universally adopted by the late 17th century, which allowed the pieces to be rolled easily back for reloading. The simple but effective elevating system of quoin and stool bed was efficient enough for use at sea. Gun tools such as worm, rammer, sponge and ladle would have been kept beside each gun, ready for action, while powder charges were brought up from the ship's magazine. A 4-pdr., the typical gun size on a small sloop or schooner, could fire a roundshot about 1,000 yards. Larger vessels such as Bartholomew Roberts' *Royal Fortune* carried a more substantial armament. Among her armament she carried four 12-pdrs., 20 8-pdrs. and a number of smaller pieces (6-pdrs. and 4-pdrs.).

By the late 17th century, naval warfare followed a standard pattern. Ships fired broadsides of roundshot at each other, and then boarded the enemy if they still refused to surrender or were badly damaged. If artillery fire was employed, pirates preferred a brief broadside, then tried to exploit the advantage of their superior numbers by boarding 'through the smoke'. In addition to roundshot, which damaged the enemy hull, chain shot (or bar shot) was fired at the enemy's rigging, which cut down the sails and with it, the ability to escape. Grapeshot was fired at close range in order to disable the enemy crew. Knowing what ammunition to load and when was vital to success in warfare at sea. It also helped avoid unnecessary damage to the potential prize.

Attack by boarding

Once the ships were alongside each other, the pirates would either fire or throw over grappling hooks to pull the two ships together. This in itself was a skill, as the vessels were likely to damage each other's rigging if they were grappled in the wrong way. The preferred method was to grapple from stern to stern, pulling the ships together at the point that ensured minimal risk to rigging and provided the largest possible area in which to fight. Once the pirates swung aboard, a fierce hand-to-hand fight would ensue. Popular weapons were muskets, blunderbusses and pistols, but swords and cutlasses would also be carried, and even pikes, axes and belaying pins! A pirate favourite was the grenade. In an action between two government sloops and a pirate vessel off Jamaica in 1718, the pirates 'threw vast numbers of powder flasks, grenado shells, and stinkpots into her which killed and wounded several and made others jump overboard'. *Grenados* (grenades) derived its name from the Spanish *granada* (pomegranate).

Pistols were the most popular firearms simply because they were so compact. Edward Teach ('Blackbeard') is reported to have carried three pairs of pistols, as well as a sword and a knife, and others carried pistols tied with silk cords to prevent them being dropped overboard during the fight. A pistol recovered from the wreck of Samuel Bellamy's pirate ship *Whydah* wrecked in 1717 was wrapped in its own long red silk looped ribbon. Although full-size military muskets were used at sea (especially by ex-privateering vessels), blunderbusses were more popular, firing a blast of scrap-iron and nails into the face of the enemy. When it came to cold steel, the most popular weapon was the cutlass. Manufactured as a cheap but effective cutting weapon, it was related to the earlier English or Scottish broadsword, or later heavy cavalry blades. Although a clumsy weapon in a confined mêlée, it was the maritime sidearm of choice. Naval officers and some merchant captains preferred the more gentlemanly smallsword. A flimsy weapon, it was designed to thrust with the point, and although effective in a confined space, it lacked the robustness of the cutlass. Other edged weapons used in boarding actions were six-foot boarding pikes, ship's axes, and hunting swords (hangers). Every seaman also carried a knife and was presumably skilled in using it.

An account of the fight between Lieutenant Maynard of the Navy and Edward Teach ('Blackbeard') illustrates the violent nature of a boarding action: 'Maynard and Teach themselves began the fight with their swords, Maynard making a thrust, the point of his sword went against Teach's cartridge box, and bended it to the hilt. Teach broke the guard of it, and wounded Maynard's fingers but did not disable him, whereupon he jumped back and threw away his sword and cut Teach's face pretty much; in the interim both companies engaged in Maynard's sloop, one of Maynard's men being a Highlander, engaged Teach with his broad sword, who gave Teach a cut on the neck, Teach saying well done lad; the Highlander replied, If it be not well done, I'll do better. With that he gave him a second stroke, which cut off his head, laying it flat on his shoulder.'

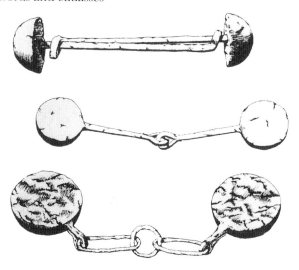

More specialist ammunition designed to cut swathes through enemy sails and rigging was found on numerous shipwrecks of the period. It was always preferable to disable a ship so it was defenceless, rather than to slug it out in a broadside engagement. The expanding barshot, split shot and chain shot were all designed to expand as far as possible, thereby cutting down more rigging in flight.

RIGHT **George Lowther, an English pirate active in the Caribbean and Atlantic seaboard between 1721-3. His ship, the** *Happy Delivery*, **is beached and being careened in the background while the crew live in tents on the shore. During the process the pirates were defenceless, and Lowther's crew were attacked and captured while careening their ship on the Venezuelan coast in 1723. Lowther escaped, but was killed soon after.**

PIRATE DENS

At various times throughout the 'golden age', piratical bases were formed, providing a safe haven to repair ships, divide plunder and hide from pursuers. The requirements were usually that a base needed to be close to shipping routes, difficult to attack and preferably containing a suitable market for the sale of stolen cargoes. The following locations all provided these facilities during the era.

Port Royal

During the latter half of the 17th century, the city of Port Royal, Jamaica, formed the main buccaneering base in the Caribbean. In its heyday it was described as a notorious den of vice, full of taverns, brothels, gambling dens and stores of plundered booty. Between 1655 and 1680, the buccaneers of Port Royal plundered hundreds of Spanish ships and raided scores of Spanish towns and cities. Peace brought an end to the buccaneering era, and a devastating earthquake in 1692 destroyed much of the city. Some observers called this 'God's punishment on this wicked city'. By the 1700s, a strong island government and increasing legitimate profits from sugar made it an unsuitable base for pirates. The Royal Navy maintained a naval base at Port Royal, and the city changed from a buccaneering den to become the base for anti-piracy operations in the Caribbean.

A map of the Caribbean and the Atlantic seaboard of America during the 'golden age of piracy'. The principal pirate den in the region was New Providence (Nassau) in the Bahamas. When the British government sent a governor to rule the island backed by naval force, the pirates were forced to disperse and find new areas of operation.

New Providence

Located close to major American and Caribbean trade routes, the island contained a good natural harbour which was difficult for large warships to enter. It was arid and sparsely settled, although it offered fresh water, timber and wild animals. This natural pirate haven was nominally the capital of the British Bahamas, and the small town there was named Nassau in 1695. Until 1717, local governors accepted bribes to leave the growing number of pirates alone. From the 1680s it had been used as a small-scale privateering and pirate base, but Spanish raids in 1703-6 made the island untenable. Peace with Spain brought the pirates back, led by Henry Jennings in 1716. By the next year over 500 pirates used the island as a base, including Edward Teach, Charles Vane, Jack Rackam and Benjamin Hornigold. The island economy thrived through trade with the

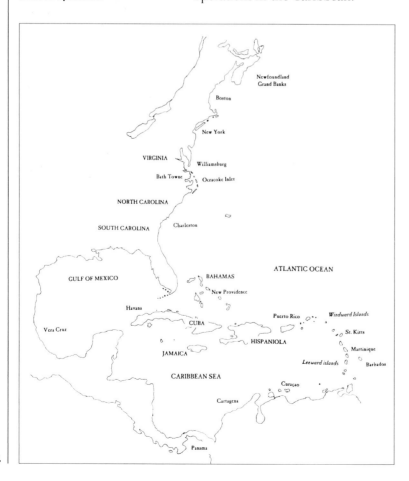

pirates, but word of the haven reached the authorities in London. The British government decided to break up the pirate base, and in July 1718 the newly appointed governor, Woodes Rogers, arrived with three warships. Many of the pirates fled, although Vane fired on the governor as he sailed away. Other pirates gave up their piratical careers. When the warships left, Rogers appointed Hornigold as his main pirate hunter, and a mass pirate hanging in December showed the world that the governor meant business. Without piracy the island returned to being a backwater, and although Woodes Rogers continued to try to develop the Bahamas, New Providence never regained its former economic vibrancy. Rogers died in Nassau in 1732.

The privateer Captain Woodes Rogers frisking Spanish ladies for jewels during their attack on the Ecuadorian port of Guayaquil in 1709. After a successful privateering career, Rogers was appointed as governor of the Bahamas, and ordered to rid the area of pirates. As a former privateer, he knew the business of piracy first hand.

The Carolinas

Although never a true pirate haven, the presence of a colonial government willing to turn a blind eye to trade with pirates made the Carolinas on the American mainland a possible successor to New Providence. When Woodes Rogers threw the pirates out of the Bahamas, the inlets and rivers of the Carolinas appeared to provide a suitable safe haven. Proximity to shipping routes and a ready local market for plunder were other important factors. Edward Teach led the way by establishing a base at Ocracoke, near Bath Towne. Subsequent piratical visitors to the area, including Stede Bonnet and Charles Vane, led to fears among ship owners that North Carolina would become a nest of pirates. Prompt action by the governors of the neighbouring colonies of Virginia and South Carolina nipped the problem in the bud. Following the death of Edward Teach and the removal of the governor of North Carolina, harsh laws were introduced preventing any trade with known pirates.

Madagascar

Madagascar in the Indian Ocean lay close to the profitable trade routes between India, the Middle East and Europe. From the 1690s, privateers of various nationalities used the island as a base, and by the end of the century it too was known as a pirate haven. With no European power willing to subdue the local population, the island was wide open, and its long coastline provided numerous suitable harbours. The end of the buccaneering era in the Caribbean prompted a growing number of mariners to relocate to the Indian Ocean. Naval expeditions in the 1690s failed to eradicate the pirate settlements, and the ejection of pirates from New Providence led to many establishing a base in Madagascar, including Christopher Condent and Edward England. By the 1720s a permanent Royal Navy presence in the Indian Ocean made piracy a risky venture. Many former pirates chose to settle on the island rather than to return home.

Woodes Rogers as governor of the Bahamas seated on the right of this painting by William Hogarth, dated 1729. His son William shows him a map of the former pirate den of New Providence Island (Nassau), which Rogers cleared of pirates in 1718. (National Maritime Museum, Greenwich, London)

PIRATE PLUNDER

Pirates rarely found ships full of coin chests. In early 18th century America and the Caribbean, coined money was in short supply, and what was in circulation was rarely standardised. Settlers brought little cash with them, and no mint was established in America until after the War of Independence. Trade between colonists and pirates such as Edward Teach brought much needed currency, and pirates found a ready market for their stolen merchandise. Coins of all nations circulated freely, and each merchant had to be his own exchange broker. Although a fictional character, a pirate in Robert Louis Stevenson's *Treasure Island* owned a notebook with a table for converting French, English and Spanish coinage, so the problem was well known. The problem was that most pirate victims didn't carry much money. Trading vessels in American or Caribbean waters carried cargoes such as sugar or rum from Jamaica, tobacco from the Carolinas, wood from Central America or manufactured goods from Europe. Other common cargoes included furs, ore, cotton, or slaves. Ships carrying substantial quantities of money were rare, and frequently well protected.

The slave trade was at its height. The triangular trade between Europe, Africa and the Americas was a highly profitable one, and attacks on slave ships could reap large rewards, depending on which leg of the voyage the ship was captured. Trade goods such as pewter or iron from England were less profitable prizes than slavers captured off the African coast, which could contain slaves, gold, ivory, and spices. Once the slaves were sold, the ship would load up with rum or sugar for her return voyage to Europe.

Every attack on a slave ship yielded a different result. Pirate crews who subscribed to the ideals of a free and democratic society might welcome Africans as equals, teaching them to become sailors. Less idealistic pirates used the Africans for labour, treating them as slaves or servants to the other seamen, but usually affording them some share of the booty. Greedier pirates felt no sympathy for their plight, and sold them to the plantations, just as their original shippers had planned. Rum was another welcome cargo. The theme of drinking is interwoven with the pirate image, and frequently the capture of vessels carrying alcohol resulted in unbridled drinking bouts.

PIRATE CAPTAINS AND CHARACTERS

Although there are too many pirates to mention in this work, it is useful to examine a number of the more prominent. This provides a useful insight into a number of areas, such as motivation, how they held a crew together, weaknesses, favoured tactics and, of course, their ultimate fate. What is instantly apparent is just how short even the most notorious pirate careers were. It also strips away many of the myths and romanticism associated with some of the more notorious characters.

Edward Teach ('Blackbeard')
Period of activity: September 1717 to November 1718 (15 months)
Probably the most famous pirate of them all, Blackbeard became a legend following his extravagant biography in Johnson's history. By ignoring John-

A group of pirates burying their treasure, a representation of a pirate group operating in the Caribbean in the early 19th century. Of particular interest is the representation of an African-American crew member. Despite its popularity in pirate fiction, accounts of pirates burying their plunder are extremely rare.

ABOVE **Edward Teach ('Black-beard'), from an engraving in an early edition of Johnson's** *Pyrates*. **His reputation as 'the devil incarnate' was probably only partly deserved, and Johnson clearly exaggerated accounts of the pirate's appearance and actions. The figure is shown carrying three brace of pistols, a Teach characteristic which can be corroborated by contemporary descriptions.**

ABOVE RIGHT **Edward Teach ('Blackbeard') with a smoking slowmatch tucked under his hat. His ship is depicted lying off Ocracoke Inlet, North Carolina, while the crew are shown unloading a stolen cargo. Teach found a ready market for plunder in the nearby settlement of Bath Towne.**

son's misleading demonic portrayal of Blackbeard and relying instead on contemporary sources, an accurate portrait can be sketched of this infamous character. A victim in 1717 described him as, 'a tall, spare man with a very black beard which he wore very long'. He was apparently broad-shouldered and, according to his nemesis Lieutenant Maynard, he tied his beard up with black ribbons. Johnson's account of him wearing a sling over his shoulders with three brace of pistols is probably accurate, given the limited effectiveness of firearms at sea in the period. A natural authority figure, Blackbeard was obviously intelligent and both socially and politically astute.

Blackbeard's real name is uncertain: Teach, Thatch or even Tache have all been used. The most common and likely version is Edward Teach. He was born in Bristol , but at some stage during his teens he took a passage to the West Indies, and served in Jamaican-based privateers during the War of Spanish Succession (1701-1714). After the war he found his way to New Providence in the Bahamas. There he encountered the pirate Benjamin Hornigold, who signed Teach on as a crewman. He learned the trade of piracy quickly, and soon set off on his own, after being given a captured slaver by Hornigold, which was renamed the *Queen Anne's Revenge*. He rapidly gained a bloodthirsty reputation. Based in New Providence, he operated in the West Indies, capturing several vessels. Johnson recorded a sea battle with the frigate HMS *Scarborough*, but there are no official records to support this. With the imminent arrival of Governor Rogers in the

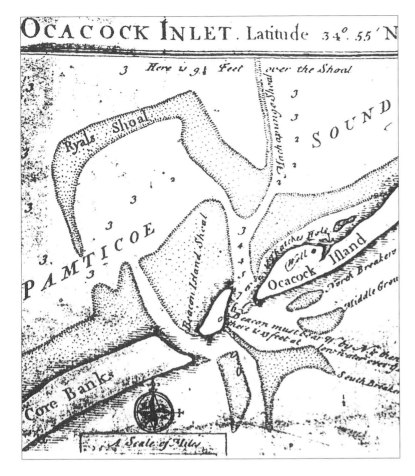

OCACOCK INLET. Latitude 34° 55'N

Ocracoke Inlet, North Carolina, showing the narrow entrance from the Atlantic (to the bottom of the map), and the network of shoals and sandbars surrounding the inlet. Beyond is the open water of Pamlico Sound. A cove marked 'Thatch's Hole' shows Teach's main anchorage and the site of his on-shore camp. (Public Record Office)

Bahamas, a new pirate base had to be found to replace New Providence.

Teach sailed for the Carolinas, arriving at Bath Towne, North Carolina, in January 1718. Establishing a base on nearby Ocracoke Island he pillaged passing ships, and found a ready market for the plundered goods in the nearby town. A bribe ensured a pardon from Governor Eden ensuring safety from prosecution. In March, the pirates sailed round Florida and cruised as far as Honduras, capturing Stede Bonnet and his sloop *Revenge* en route. Adding more vessels to his squadron, he plundered several more ships before returning north. His crew numbered over 400 men. In May 1718 Teach blockaded Charleston, South Carolina, plundering eight vessels and capturing, then ransoming a prominent citizen in return for a chest of medical supplies. It was rumoured that the crew were suffering from a form of venereal disease. He then returned to Bath Towne, but lost the *Queen Anne's Revenge* on a sandbar.

Teach sold his plunder, bought a house and was granted another pardon by Governor Eden. The governor even rigged the local Admiralty courts, who recognised Teach as the owner of the vessels he had captured during his cruise. However, resentment of this legitimised piracy was growing, and ship owners feared that the area would become an established pirate haven. When Charles Vane visited Teach in October, these fears increased. Complaints reached the neighbouring colony of Virginia, and the governor, Alexander Spotswood, vowed to flush out the pirate nest. As the waters around Teach's base at Ocracoke were too shallow for large naval vessels, Spotswood hired two sloops out of his own pocket, filling them with Royal Naval crews from HMS *Pearl* and HMS *Lyme*, both anchored in the James River. Lieutenant Maynard of the Royal Navy was placed in command, 'an experienced officer and a gentleman of great bravery and resolution'.

Arriving off Ocracoke Inlet, Maynard attacked at dawn on Friday 22 November 1718. Many of the pirates were away in Bath Towne, so with 60 men, Maynard's crew outnumbered the pirates by over three to one. Teach had one sloop, the *Adventure*, which, unlike the unnamed attacking ships, carried nine guns, and tried to escape through the shallows. In their hurry to pursue, the naval sloops ran aground. According to Maynard's account Teach yelled, 'Rank Damnation to me and my men, whom he stil'd

Cowardly Puppies, saying he would neither give nor take Quarter'. The sloops freed themselves with the rising tide and rowed in pursuit. Teach turned and fired a broadside of grapeshot, killing the midshipman in command of the sloop *Ranger*, and killing or wounding several of her crew. Maynard in the *Jane* fired a bow chaser at the *Adventure*, and a shot cut her jib, forcing her aground. Maynard had hidden most of his men below decks, and Teach decided to board the naval sloop. He came alongside, and as he did the naval crew swarmed on deck. A vicious mêlée ensued, and Maynard and Teach fought each other face-to-face. Maynard wounded Teach with a pistol shot, but broke his own sword, giving Teach the upper hand. Maynard was saved by a Scotsman who decapitated the pirate. The mêlée continued until all the pirates were killed or had surrendered.

Maynard sailed to Bath Towne, repaired his ships and sailed back to Williamsburg, dangling Teach's head from the bowsprit of his sloop. In the subsequent trial, 13 pirates were convicted and hanged, while two were acquitted or reprieved.

Jack (or John) Rackam ('Calico Jack') gained his nickname from the bright cotton clothing he sometimes wore. A small-time pirate, his main claim to fame was as the lover of the female pirate Anne Bonny. Rackam was hanged in Port Royal, Jamaica, in 1720.

Anne Bonny, Mary Reade and Jack Rackam ('Calico Jack')

Period of activity: July 1718 to November 1720 (29 months)

'Calico Jack' was typical of the small-time pirates whose small sloops preyed on coastal shipping. Little is known of his origins, but by 1718 he had somehow made his way to New Providence Island. He served with Vane, fleeing the island when Vane escaped from the new governor, Woodes Rogers. By the spring of 1719 he was elected as quartermaster, and became Vane's deputy. Soon after, a quarrel broke out among the crew, and Rackam replaced Vane as a pirate captain. Vane was put ashore, and Rackam continued Vane's cruise in two sloops.

According to some accounts the vessels were both lost when a Jamaican-based patrol sloop captured them while most of the crew were ashore. Rackam returned to New Providence, and in May 1719 he was granted a pardon by Governor Rogers as

The pair of female pirates, Anne Bonny (left) and Mary Reade (right). Never more than a minor nuisance, the trio of Bonny, Reade and Rackam were famous more for their relationship than their deeds.

part of Rogers' general pirate amnesty. It was there that he met Anne Bonny. Law-abiding life ashore proved unpalatable, and in August 1719 Rackam stole a sloop named the *William*, and returned to piracy. His crew included the female pirates Bonny and Mary Reade. Based in Bahamian waters, he cruised between Bermuda and Hispaniola, capturing several ships and a number of profitable cargoes. He then sailed around Cuba attacking local craft, before reaching the north coast of Jamaica. There his luck ran out. While at anchor off the western tip of the island, he was surprised by a sloop belonging to the governor of Jamaica. Most of Rackam's nine male crew were drunk, but according to testimonies the women roused them into action. The *William* cut her anchor cable and fled, but was overhauled by the Jamaican sloop during the night. The ships exchanged fire, and then Captain Barnet led a boarding party onto the deck of the pirate vessel. Bonny and Reade were the only members of the crew who offered any kind of resistance. Rackam himself was apparently too drunk to defend himself. The women were overcome, and the pirates were taken to Port Royal to stand trial.

The background of the female pirates was recorded by contemporaries during the trial, which caused a sensation throughout Europe and the Americas. The excitement largely stemmed from the revelation that they had lived as men for years, escaping the traditional restrictions imposed on the lives of contemporary women. In other words, they were not only female pirates, but they broke society's strict rules. Their backgrounds were probably embroidered by Johnson, but his account was gleaned from contemporary press reports. Mary Reade's mother apparently 'bred her

LEFT **Anne Bonny, the lover of Jack Rackam. She is depicted bearing her breasts (to prove her sex), and is shown wearing a seaman's jacket and canvas trousers. Both Bonny and Reade wore men's clothing when at sea.**

Charles Vane became notorious when he defied Woodes Rogers, the new governor of the Bahamas, in the harbour of New Providence in 1718. Subsequently he was voted out of his captaincy, shipwrecked, and then captured by a passing ship. According to Johnson, when hanged he 'showed not the least remorse for the crimes of his past life'.

daughter dressed as a boy', and after serving as a man in domestic service, on a warship and also in the British army, she fell in love and married a soldier. When he died she reverted to her 'male' role and took passage as a seaman on a Caribbean-bound ship. Captured by pirates in 1717, she joined them, and through them met Rackam's companion, Anne Bonny.

According to contemporary sources, Anne Bonny was raised as a boy to fulfil the requirements of a will, although she retained her feminine character. When she left home she married a seaman, who subsequently turned to piracy. Her husband used New Providence as his base, and there she met Mary Reade, although accounts contradict each other as to the nature of their first encounter. In any event, the women became friends, which is not surprising, given their similar and unusual backgrounds. In New Providence she met Rackam, who persuaded her to abandon her husband. The women were tried separately from their fellow pirates because of the notoriety of their case. In court it was reported that 'they were both very profligate, cursing and swearing much, and very ready and willing to do anything'. Victims testified that they donned men's clothing when in action, but otherwise dressed as women. Following the trial, both women were sentenced to death, but were reprieved when it was discovered that they were both pregnant. Mary died subsequently in a Jamaican prison in 1721, but Anne's fate is unknown.

Charles Vane

Period of activity: July 1718 to November 1720 (28 months)

Charles Vane took to piracy in 1716, and served as part of Henry Jennings' crew. A Spanish treasure fleet had been wrecked on the eastern coast of Florida in 1715, and during 1716 Jennings raided the camps of the salvagers, capturing large quantities of silver. Originally based in Jamaica, Jennings found that his illegal attacks made his presence unwelcome. He moved to New Providence in 1717, and when Governor Woodes Rogers took up residence in 1718, he accepted a pardon, settling down to live off his plunder. In this respect Jennings was one of the more successful pirates. Charles Vane was not so fortunate.

Just before Rogers arrived, Vane made his first independent cruise, capturing a French merchant vessel. When the new governor appeared in August 1718, Vane knew he would either have to give up his plunder or flee New Providence. He set fire to the French vessel, sailing it straight for Rogers' flagship. As the warship carrying Rogers was busy avoiding the fireship, Vane and his pirate crew sailed by in their barquentine, firing at the Royal Naval frigate and jeering. Vane escaped in the confusion, taking his plunder with him. Vessels were sent after him, but Vane eluded them,

23

When the crews of Edward Teach ('Blackbeard') and Charles Vane met at Ocracoke Inlet, North Carolina, in 1718, they held a week-long celebration, and were joined by women and traders from the nearby settlement of Bath Towne. This 19th century engraving depicts the festivities.

OPPOSITE BELOW **Henry Every shown wielding a cutlass and armed with two brace of pistols. In the background the engraving depicts the fight between Every's ship the *Fancy*, and the treasure ship of the Great Moghul, the *Gang-i-sawai*.**

although they caught a number of other runaway pirates. Subsequently, Vane and his crew bore a grudge against the Bahamas and their governor, and attacked New Providence shipping while passing by in the spring of 1719. Vane then headed for the Carolinas, capturing a sloop which he used as a second ship, and taking a number of prizes. The sloop's crew promptly deserted, the first indications of bad blood between Vane and his men. A number of naval vessels were sent in pursuit by Governor Spotswood of Virginia during late August and early September 1718, but he evaded them. The same ships, however, managed to capture the pirate Stede Bonnet and his crew, who were operating in the same waters.

While operating off the North Carolina coast Vane met up with Edward Teach and his crew at their Ocracoke base. The two crews celebrated their union by holding a drunken party; a sort of pirate convention. By October he set sail again, this time heading north towards New York, taking ships along the way. Operating off Long Island in November, he captured a growing tally of ships before heading back to the Carolinas to sell the cargoes.

He returned to the Caribbean in early 1719, this time operating in the Windward passage between Cuba and Hispaniola. His squadron now consisted of two vessels. In March 1719 a quarrel broke out among the crew over an alleged incident of cowardice on Vane's part, and his shipmates elected Jack Rackam as captain instead. Vane was given a small captured sloop and sent on his way with the few remaining crew who remained loyal to him. Starting from scratch again, he succeeded in capturing a couple of small ships before running into a hurricane in the Bay of Honduras. His ship ran aground, and Vane with one other survivor were stranded on a small island for several months before being rescued by a passing ship. One of the rescuers recognised Vane, and the pirates were locked up, shipped to Port Royal, Jamaica, and put on trial. Both Vane and his one surviving crewman were found guilty and hanged in November 1720.

Henry Every ('Long Ben')

Period of activity: June 1694 to September 1695 (15 months)

Little is known of Every's early life, although in the early 1690s he served aboard a slave ship. Accounts of an early piratical career based in the Bahamas appears unfounded. In 1694 he was serving as the first mate on a privateer named the *Charles*, licensed by the Spanish to operate against the French colony of Martinique. He engineered a mutiny, took over the ship and was elected captain. Renaming the vessel the *Fancy*, the pirates crossed to the African coast, then sailed south, capturing four vessels, including a French pirate vessel returning home with her spoils. Off the Cape of Good Hope Every wrote an open letter to the English papers, proclaiming his loyalty to England and Holland. It also focused attention on his exploits.

Henry Every, arguably the most successful pirate of them all. After capturing a treasure ship in the Indian Ocean, he returned home, changed his identity and disappeared. He was never recaptured by the authorities, and his success proved an inspiration to other would-be pirates.

Entering the Indian Ocean, he found the waters around the Red Sea full of pirates, and Every temporarily bonded a group of them into a fleet. Together, they were powerful enough to intercept the well-armed treasure convoys which sailed annually between India and the Middle East. When they saw the approaching pirates, most of the Moghul of India's fleet fled, and nightfall covered their escape. Every was lucky, and when dawn broke he found two ships within range. The smaller one, the *Fateh Mohammed*, was quickly overcome, but the larger, the *Gang-i-sawai*, only surrendered after a tough, two-hour fight. Survivors were killed, tortured to reveal hidden caches of treasure and women passengers raped. The brutality was in keeping with the era, especially given the religious and racial differences between victor and vanquished.

Once the smoke cleared, Every and his crew found they had captured the fleet's main treasure ship, containing over £600,000 of gold, silver and jewels. Each pirate in the fleet received a share estimated at over £1,000, or over 80 years' worth of the average seaman's wages at the time!

The fleet disbanded, and the *Fancy* sailed back to the Caribbean. In New Providence, the governor of the Bahamas offered protection in return for an immense bribe. While many of his crew returned to England, only to be apprehended and hanged, Every sailed for Ireland, then vanished into obscurity.

Known as the 'Arch Pirate', he was the only successful pirate who survived to live off his plunder. Sightings were common over the next few decades, but none proved to be accurate. His success also encouraged others to follow in his footsteps.

Stede Bonnet

Period of activity: March 1717 to November 1718 (20 months)

According to Johnson's history, Stede Bonnet was an ex-army major and Barbados plantation owner who turned to piracy in 1717. Unfortunately, no record of him can be found among the Barbadian archives. Johnson records that he actually purchased his own ship, the sloop *Revenge* of 10 guns, crewed it with piratical volunteers and sailed for the Carolinas. Operating off the Atlantic seaboard, he captured and plundered several ships from New York down to the Carolinas, before he wintered in North Carolina, careening his ship and housing his crew ashore. In the spring he headed south towards the Gulf of Honduras, but en route in March 1718 he ran into Edward Teach with a larger ship and crew. Bonnet surrendered and was taken along as a virtual prisoner. Teach reportedly laughed at the pirate gentleman while he took his ship from him!

By June 1718 he was released with his sloop off the North Carolina coast, and hearing that the newly formed Great Britain was at war with Spain, he approached the pirate-friendly governor of North Carolina for a pardon. He got it, and officially set off towards the Virgin Islands to act as a privateer, with a Letter of Marque to prey on Spanish shipping. He still bore a grudge against Teach, and tried to hunt him down, but soon gave up the quest. He then changed the name of his ship to the *Royal James* and adopted an assumed name (Captain Thomas), before reverting to his chosen career of piracy. When lying in the Cape Fear River undergoing repairs, he captured a local ship, and word reached the city authorities at Charleston, South Carolina. A local ship owner, William Rhett, was authorised to attack the pirates with two sloops. In October 1718 the Charleston sloops found the pirate lair and attacked Bonnet, who retreated up the river. Running aground, he was forced to fight. After a five-hour exchange of fire, Bonnet and the surviving crew surrendered. The pirates were taken to Charleston, a city still smarting from their treatment by Teach. While imprisoned in a private house, Bonnet escaped, but was quickly recaptured. He was found guilty and hanged in November 1718, along with 30 of his crew. A pirate turned informant and four others were acquitted.

The 'gentleman pirate' Stede Bonnet being hanged at Charleston Harbour in November 1718. The penitent pirate is shown holding a sprig of nosegay, signifying forgiveness, as sailors and townspeople look on. Until the last moment he expected to be pardoned by the governor of South Carolina.

William Kidd

Period of activity: May 1697 to April 1700 (35 months)

William Kidd is one of the better known pirates, more for his fate than his actions. He only made one voyage and took only one significant prize but it was enough to bring him to trial and cause a major political scandal. His inclusion here is more because of this subsequent fame than because of his deeds.

Before he turned to piracy, the Scottish-born Kidd served in a privateering vessel in the Caribbean. Kidd settled in New York, but in 1695 he sailed to England, hoping to win more extensive privateering contracts. Once there he met Richard, Earl of Bellamont, newly appointed governor of New York and Massachusetts. Bellamont soon talked Kidd into a plan involving semi-legal privateering, to be conducted by Kidd in a specially built vessel, acting on behalf of financial backers. These backers included Bellamont and other influential politicians. They bought Kidd the *Adventure Galley* of 34 guns and presented him with a contract and a Letter of Marque against the French and against pirates. It was implied the backers would also turn a blind eye to the odd piratical act if it turned a profit. The contract was financially restrictive, meaning Kidd would receive little financial gain for his efforts, and the crew would receive even less. Most of the money was earmarked for the backers. The terms strongly influenced the subsequent actions of Kidd and his crew.

Kidd sailed in May 1696, heading first to New York to sign on a crew of old privateering hands, then crossed the Atlantic to West Africa. He sailed into the Indian Ocean, and in April 1697 signed on more crew in Madagascar and turned to piracy. In August he attacked East India Company ships but was driven off. Another skirmish with Portuguese warships proved uneventful, and after snapping up a small English prize, Kidd retired to the Laccadive Islands for repairs. By November he was at sea again, but ran away from a couple of potential victims who seemed too well armed. An argument with the ship's gunner led to Kidd killing the man, and any poten-

William Kidd in a portrait by an unknown artist, supposedly painted while Kidd stood trial. It was based on a sketch drawn during the trial, and has been attributed to Sir James Thornbull. Scraps of the clothes worn by Kidd at the gallows are pinned to the lower left corner. (Private Collection)

William Kidd burying his family bible near Plymouth before undertaking a career of piracy. This 1837 illustration depicts one of the many fictitious events which obscure the true story of Captain Kidd.

Richard Coote, Earl of Bellamont, governor of New York and Massachusetts, c.1695. In that year Bellamont met Kidd and struck a deal that would lead Kidd to the gallows. Bellamont's assurance of protection was revoked when Kidd arrived back from the Indian Ocean. (British Museum)

RIGHT **The inventory of Kidd's plunder as drawn up in Boston between William Kidd and the Earl of Bellamont in July 1699. The governor distrusted Kidd, whom he thought had hidden a further large portion of his booty. The haul includes silver ingots, gold pieces, rare jewels and other more usual forms of cargo.**

OPPOSITE BELOW **The Guinea Coast (West Africa), c.1720. This region was the centre of the slave trade, and provided particularly lucrative pickings for pirates during the era. It was the favoured cruising ground of Bartholomew Roberts, who almost single-handedly brought the slave trade to a halt.**

tial mutiny was quelled. After attacking a handful of small prizes, Kidd came upon the *Queddah Merchant* in January 1698. Capturing her and splitting the booty, Kidd abandoned the rotten *Adventure Galley* and shifted into the prize, which he renamed the *Adventure Prize*. The East India Company forced the government to brand Kidd as a pirate, and any potential pardon was now politically impossible. It also meant his backers could not support him.

Now a wanted man, Kidd sailed back to the Caribbean, then on to Boston, where he tried to make a deal with Governor Bellamont. He was promptly arrested on Bellamont's orders in April 1700 and shipped to England in chains. Thrown into prison, he was now a political pawn. The opposition tried to make Kidd indict his secret government backers, and Kidd testified in Parliament. The government narrowly avoided a political disaster by 'losing' incriminating documents, and the case was dropped. To the British government, Kidd remained a dangerous liability. In May 1701 after a heavily rigged trial, he was found guilty of murdering his former gunner and of piracy. He was hanged at Execution Dock in Wapping, and his body hung in a cage on the banks of the River Thames as a warning to would-be pirates. Rumours that he buried his loot on Long Island before entering New York were probably true, although Governor Bellamont recovered most of the plunder soon after Kidd was arrested. He was the only figure to profit from Kidd's pirate career.

Bartholomew Roberts ('Black Bart')

Period of activity: June 1719 to February 1722 (30 months)

Bartholomew Roberts was born in South Wales and originally called John Roberts . In June 1719, while serving as the mate of a merchant slaver, his ship was captured by another Welshman, the pirate Howell Davis. Davis in his turn had chosen a career of piracy when he was captured by Edward England. Roberts joined Davis' crew and when Davis was killed in a skirmish, Roberts was elected captain. Changing his first name to Bartholomew to cover his tracks, he quickly earned the nickname 'Black Bart'.

After cruising in West African waters, he sailed for Brazil. Coming across a Portuguese convoy, he captured a number of ships including a warship. Roberts took his growing fleet to the American colonies. Selling ships and cargo in New England, he plundered the fishing grounds of Newfoundland in the summer of 1720, capturing dozens of vessels and destroying numerous others. Trading captured ships for a 28-gun French ship which he renamed *Royal Fortune*, he sailed south along the American coastline, capturing more merchantmen on the way. When he reached the Caribbean in the late summer of 1720, he captured 15 French and English ships, as well as a well-armed Dutch ship carrying 42 guns, in a four-day spree. An

Bartholomew Roberts ('Black Bart'), the most prolific ship-capturing pirate of the era. His tally of over 200 ships came to an end when he was killed in action off the West African coast in 1723. Renowned as an elegant dresser, he reputedly wore a red waistcoat, a feathered hat and a jewelled cross around his neck.

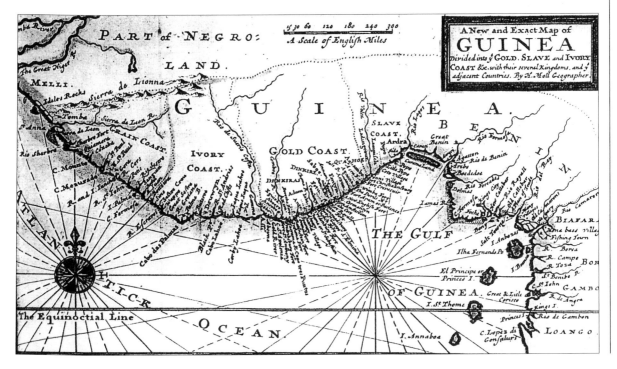

attempt at a transatlantic voyage was foiled by poor winds and faulty navigation, so by the autumn the pirates had returned to the West Indies. Attacks on St Kitts and Martinique netted a further haul of ships, and the rampage continued until the spring of 1721. In the process, Roberts managed to capture a sworn enemy, the governor of Martinique, who was promptly hanged from the yardarm of his own ship. The 52-gun French warship which carried him was pressed into service and renamed the *Royal Fortune* (as were most of Roberts' large prizes). He eventually returned to the African coast, where he captured several merchant slavers during the summer of 1721. The Royal Africa Company's ship *Onslow* became the last ship renamed *Royal Fortune*. Roberts continued to cruise off Liberia and

The death warrant for 19 members of Bartholomew Roberts' crew, following a mass trial in Cape Coast Castle, Guinea. In all, 57 pirates were hanged outside the castle, the largest pirate execution of the 18th century.

Nigeria, capturing scores of slave ships. A Royal naval force was despatched to track down the pirates, and, on 10 February 1722, Captain Ogle of HMS *Swallow* caught up with the *Royal Fortune*.

The pirates were at anchor off Cape Lopez, after having captured prizes the day before, and (apparently) having celebrated with a drinking spree. The morning after brought a well-armed naval frigate at action stations as well as a hangover. Roberts had to pass Ogle's ship in order to escape, and steered for the warship, while his crew scrambled to prepare their ship for action. As the ships passed, the *Swallow* fired a broadside of grapeshot at point-blank range. Roberts was killed instantly. His crew threw his body overboard still clad in all his finery, including a splendid jewelled cross, partly to avoid the corpse being captured. The ships continued to exchange broadsides in a running battle. After three hours, the surviving pirates surrendered. Two other ships of the pirate fleet were also captured, along with a haul of 300 tons of gold dust.

In what was the largest pirate trial and execution of the era, the survivors were tried and executed at Cape Coast Castle, in West Africa.

Roberts' boldness was his trademark. He led his crew into action wearing a brace of pistols tucked into a silk bandoleer and carrying a sharp cutlass. He attacked ships of all nations, but particularly singled out France and its colonies – he hanged the governor of Martinique, and reportedly tortured and killed French prisoners. A tall, handsome man who loved fine clothes, he was a teetotaller, a rarity among sailors of the period. He was also a gifted leader of men, and held his crews together by the use of prize money, codes of conduct and above all, constant success. Among the pirates who were hanged was Roberts' lover, John Walden. Although called 'Miss Nanny' behind his back, Walden was a tough character, who was accused of burning slaves alive during the trial. Roberts' career has been upheld as one of the most successful and flamboyant of the pirate era. He was one of the most prosperous pirates of all time, following 'the pirate round' from Africa to the Americas and back again, capturing more than 200 ships in the process.

PIRATE SHIPS

The pirate ship performed several roles. The crew had to be fed and kept in readiness. It was also the storeroom for plunder. As pirate crews were larger than those on merchant vessels, space was often at a premium. The ship provided the means to attack, so it had to be well armed. It was also the sole means of escape, so speed was vital, or as Johnson wrote, it acted as 'a light pair of heels being of great use either to take, or to escape being taken'. It is difficult to find a contemporary representation of a pirate ship. Pirates altered captured vessels to suit their particular needs, so it is sensible to examine the types of craft they acquired. Traditionally a 'ship' refers to a vessel with three masts and a full suite of square-rigged sails. Very few pirate vessels were 'ships' in the truest sense.

Judging by statistics, most pirates stole their craft during an attack, or acquired them through a mutiny. Their ships were often deemed unsuitable, and the vessel was abandoned after the capture of something better. Another source of pirate ships were the vessels fitted out as privateers. When their privateering contract ended, the crew often turned to piracy.

Many pirates retained one ship for their whole (often brief) piratical career, although a few exchanged ships several times. Bartholomew Roberts changed ships six times during his career, renaming each one the *Royal Fortune*. When ships were captured they were either sold, destroyed or turned into pirate vessels themselves.

The business of privateering created the need for specialised fast, well-armed vessels, and during the War of Spanish Succession (1700-1714) large numbers were produced. For English privateers, once peace was declared, the crews often saw no alternative but to turn to piracy. The advantage of privateering vessels was their suitability to pirate needs. After all, privateering was simply legitimised piracy. They made excellent pirate vessels without the need of much conversion. Not all privateers turned to piracy, and frequently ex-privateer sloops were hired by colonial governors as pirate hunters.

Pirates preferred small, fast vessels such as sloops, brigantines and schooners. Sloops produced in the Caribbean were ideally suited to the needs of pirate crews, although a number of pirate crews preferred roomier, larger vessels. As well as speed, smaller vessels had an advantage in draft. They could enter shallow waters without fear of grounding, waters where larger vessels were unable to follow. Smaller vessels were also easier to maintain and careen, an important factor if speed was to be maintained. Careening involved beaching the vessel and scraping and cleaning the lower hulls.

If a ship needed to be converted, the aim was to alter her 'making such alterations as might fit her for a Sea Rover, pulling down her bulkheads, and making her flush, so that she became, in all respects, as complete a ship for their purpose as any they could have found' (Johnson). By removing unnecessary internal partitions below decks, they created a clear

A colonial American schooner of the 18th century. A sloop was essentially a single-masted version of the schooner. Both types proved popular with pirates because of their speed and shallow draught. Drawing by Henry Rush.

space to work the vessel's guns, as was the case in warships. 'Making her flush' involved removing the forecastle and lowering the quarter-deck so that the weather deck (upper deck) continued from bow to stern. This created an unobstructed fighting platform. The hull might also be pierced to carry extra guns, her timbers strengthened to absorb the greater stresses created by the increased armament, and she would be fitted with an array of swivel guns mounted on the gunwales.

CAPTAIN KIDD, 1700

A

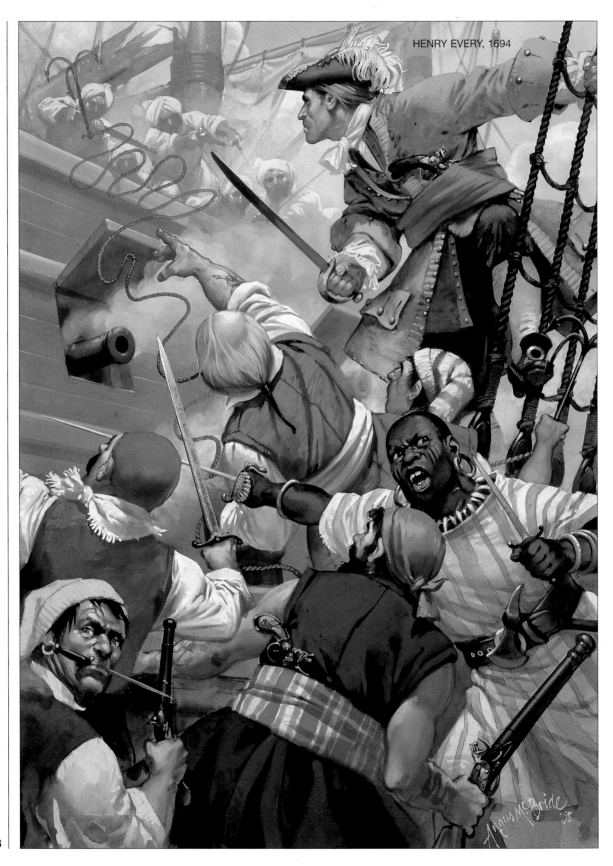

HENRY EVERY, 1694

B

GOVERNOR ROGERS ENTERING NEW PROVIDENCE, 1718

C

GUN AND CREW, EARLY EIGHTEENTH CENTURY

D

1. Anne Bonny
2. Mary Reade, 1720

E

F

BLACKBEARD'S LAST FIGHT, 1718

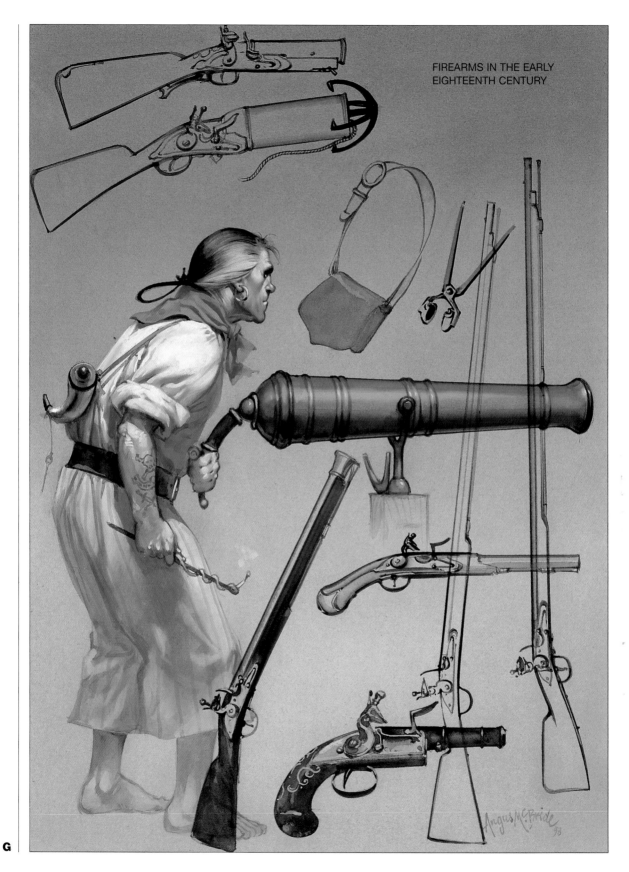

FIREARMS IN THE EARLY
EIGHTEENTH CENTURY

STEDE BONNET'S EXECUTION, 1718

BARTHOLOMEW ROBERTS, 1723

EDGED WEAPONS IN THE EARLY EIGHTEENTH CENTURY

J

PIRATE FLAGS:
1. **Edward Teach (Blackbeard)**
2. **Stede Bonnet**
3. **"Calico" Jack Rackam**
4. **Edward Low**
5. **Christopher Moody**
6. **Henry Every**
7. **Bartholomew Roberts**
8. **Bartholomew Roberts**
9. **Edward England**

Sloops

During the early 18th century 'sloop' described a wide range of vessels and formed the largest single type of craft encountered in the Caribbean. Sloops were usually small, single-masted craft, carrying a huge spread of sail in proportion to their size. This made them fast and manoeuvrable, and their shallow draught and fast lines made them ideal as small pirate ships. Their sail arrangement was normally a fore-and-aft rig, with a mainsail and a single foresail. (At the time 'sloop' also referred to similar small vessels with one, two or three masts.)

Typical pirate sloops could carry up to 75 men and 14 guns. Jamaican shipbuilders produced a particularly highly regarded form of sloop, with a reputation for speed and seaworthiness. Traditionally, Jamaican sloops were built using red cedar, giving them a distinctive hull colour. Bermudan sloops and schooners had a similar reputation. A variant of the sloop was the cutter, which was a small single-masted vessel with a fore-and-aft mainsail, a foresail and a jib. It also frequently carried a square-rigged topsail. Cutters were traditionally employed by the navy or colonial authorities, who used them as pirate hunters.

Schooners

An American variation of the sloop, the 'schooner' became increasingly common as the 18th century wore on. Schooners were usually defined as being two-masted ships carrying fore and aft sails on both masts. Their narrow hulls and large spread of sail made them fast, capable of exceeding 11 knots in the right conditions. They also had a shallow draught, allowing pirate vessels to hide amid shallow waters and shoals. Weighing up to 100 tons, pirate schooners could carry around 75 men and eight guns. Their disadvantage for pirates was that they had a limited cruising range, and were forced to put in to port to take on water and supplies. The alternative was to take what was needed from other vessels, making success a prerequisite for a pirate captain.

The hull plan and lines of the schooner depicted on p.32. A particular characteristic of the schooner was the sharp rake to the two masts, and the peculiarly American hull form was prized by privateers for its sailing qualities.

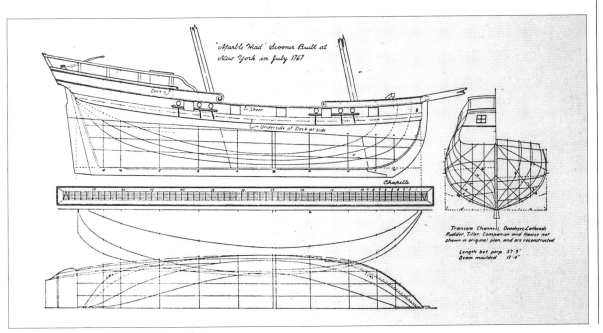

Brigantines

Another form of vessel commonly found in American waters, the brigantine had foremasts which carried square-rigged sails, while their mainmasts used a fore-and-aft rigged mainsail, and a square-rigged topsail. This sail combination allowed the brigantine to take advantage of different wind conditions. They measured up to 80 feet long, weighed up to 150 tons and could carry up to 100 men and 12 guns.

A variant of the brigantine, the brig was not so common in American or Caribbean waters. It was a fully square-rigged two-masted vessel, although it sometimes used an additional fore-and-aft sail between the two masts. Another variant was the snow, who had her spanker (the gaff-rigged sail at the back of the mainmast) set on a separate spar extension of the mainmast (the trysail). The Royal Navy employed a number of snows as patrol vessels in pirate-infested waters.

Three-masted vessels (Square-Riggers)

These were true ships, three-masted vessels with a full suite of square sails. Mariners reserved the term 'merchant ship' for vessels of this type. Although slower than the smaller vessels used by pirates, these did have certain advantages. They were usually more seaworthy, provided better gun platforms and could hold a larger crew than sloops. A number of pirates, including Bartholomew Roberts and Charles Vane, preferred large square-rigged ships.

Three-masted square-rigged merchant ships could also remain at sea for extended periods. Edward Teach's *Queen Anne's Revenge* was a three-masted ex-slave ship, converted to carry 40 guns, making her as powerful as any naval vessel of a similar size. A normal merchant ship of around 300 tons would carry no more than 16 guns, although they rarely carried the crew to operate more than a fraction of them. Three-masted warships started at 6th rates (carrying from 12 to 24 guns), and continued up from there. As a 5th rate frigate carried up to 40 guns, it was usually more than a match for any pirate vessel careless enough to be drawn within range of her guns. The exception were ships like Roberts' *Royal Fortune* or Teach's *Queen Anne's Revenge*, which carried a similar armament.

RIGHT **The pirate crew of Thomas Anstis holding a mock trial while ashore on Cuba, 1721. Crewmen dressed as judges and bailiffs question a pirate captive with a noose around his neck. Anstis and his crew deserted from Bartholomew Roberts in 1721. After killing Anstis in 1723, most of his crew surrendered to the Dutch authorities on Curacao.**

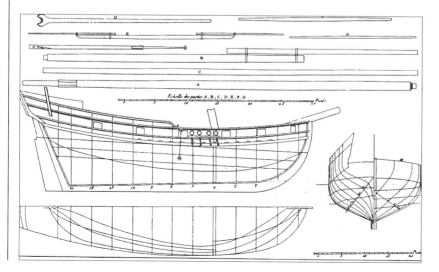

The hull plan and lines of a Bermudan sloop, from Chapman's *Architectura Navalis Mercatoria* (1768). Sloops such as this accounted for the majority of pirate vessels operating in the Caribbean during the early 18th century.

A selection of Pirate Ship Names

Some ship names were used by more than one pirate, and some pirates, such as Bartholomew Roberts, renamed their ships several times. Also, some pirates were associated with several ships during their careers. Only the most important ones are recorded here. Ships were often renamed with various names, and the names used indiscriminately. Roberts had a ship called the *Fortune* which was renamed the *Happy Fortune*, and later *Royal Fortune*. Changing names was also a means of avoiding identification, or was undertaken as a form of camouflage.

Pirate Ship	Associated Captain
Adventure Galley	William Kidd
Fancy	Henry Every, Edward England
Flying Dragon	Edmund Condent
Happy Delivery	George Lowther
Liberty	Thomas Tew
Pearl	Edward England
Queen Anne's Revenge	Edward Teach (Blackbeard)
Ranger	Charles Vane
Revenge	John Gow, Stede Bonnet, John Phillips, Edward Teach
Rising Sun	William Moody
Royal Fortune	Bartholomew Roberts
Whydah	Samuel Bellamy

PIRATE CODES

The popular image of pirates is one of a lawless group of cut-throats, operating beyond the fringes of society. While elements of this are correct, they were also frequently well organised, at least in terms of self-imposed legal codes and charters. Piracy in the early 18th century actually provided an example of experimental democracy in action, long before such notions became popular. In most recorded cases, a pirate vessel was owned and operated by the crew themselves, who conducted themselves according to rules laid out to control most aspects of their piratical activity. The division of plunder was agreed to and laid out, officers were elected, codes of discipline enforced and punishments spelled out, all imposed by the crew on themselves. Rather than an anarchic body, a pirate crew, although having immense individual freedom, were constrained by a code of conduct, in a way similar to the articles employed on contemporary merchant or naval ships.

Every pirate ship followed its own set of rules (or articles) that were actually written up and agreed to by all parties before the cruise ever started. If the crew of a merchant ship mutinied and turned to piracy, this was often the first action after taking over the ship. The precedent for this had been set in the preceding century. In the late 17th century, buccaneers had used a form of written charter (or 'Charte-Partie'), outlining conditions of service, restitution in case of death or injury and the agreed division of any booty. This was considered a legal document, and was even used in Jamaican courts to settle disputes. As buccaneering gave way to piracy in the late 17th century, these became more like secret charters than legal documents. A number of different examples have been preserved. Some, such as those drawn up by Bartholomew Roberts and his crew, were quite draconian, but all provide a rare and useful insight into the pirate's life at sea. Whatever form it took, the articles were rigidly adhered to. The pirates had to turn their backs on the law of nations, and the near-absolute

The crew of Bartholomew Roberts indulging in a drinking bout while ashore on the banks of the Old Calabar River, in West Africa. Rum drinking played a major part in the pirate routine, and also led to the capture or death of Roberts and his crew in 1723.

power granted to captains at sea. To replace them they set about establishing their own egalitarian form of constitution and surviving examples all follow a similar pattern.

The captain was usually elected into office by the crew, often by a majority show of hands. He could just as easily be voted out if the crew became dissatisfied with his performance. He had complete authority when the ship was in action, much as was the case on naval vessels. He could kill a crew member who refused to follow orders, and made all the decisions without question.

When the smoke cleared, the quartermaster took over the division of the spoils. The only other elected officer, the quartermaster, shared power with the captain and was his second-in-command. His duties included supervising the running of the ship, except when in battle, and he decided what plunder to take, which captured ships to keep and which should be burned. He was in charge of everything of value taken from a captured ship, which he placed in a common fund until it was divided. He then supervised its distribution and resolved any arguments which arose. The majority of pirates had previously served on warships, and the absolute power of a naval captain was an anathema to them. Their solution was this form of power sharing between captain and quartermaster. Like the captain, the quartermaster could be removed from power at any time by a majority vote.

In most cases, the other officers on board a pirate ship were appointed by the captain (or by both captain and quartermaster). The master (or sailing master) was responsible for navigation, and was a valued member of the crew (often being the only literate person on board). The boatswain was in charge of all seamanship tasks, as well as maintaining the ship, the sails, rigging and tackle. The gunner supervised the gun crews and maintained the ship's armament and all communally held small arms. Other posts included the sailmaker and ship's carpenter, and occasionally larger vessels

(including many ex-privateers) employed a surgeon of sorts.

The division of plunder was always a possible area of contention among a pirate crew, so the process was recorded in detail. If a number of ships were operating in consort (as was the case with Bartholomew Roberts' fleet in 1722), the plunder was divided equally between all the ships, in proportion to the crew carried. This aimed to reduce the chance of any one ship absconding with all the loot. The booty was normally divided at the end of a voyage. Before it was split, deductions were made to men who had suffered injury, following a pre-arranged rate. Unlike the prize money of naval service, the ship's officers received at most two shares to the average crewman's one. In the Royal Navy, a captain could keep up to a quarter, depending on circumstance). Unlike the buccaneering era, where captured goods frequently included hauls of specie, the usual pirate hauls of sugar, cloth, rum or tobacco were harder to divide. The romanticised view of the crew sitting on a beach dividing up chests full of treasure is a fantasy. More commonly, the cargo would be sold to a known 'middle man' in a secluded inlet or small port. The income would then be divided by the quartermaster. If this was impossible, a rough division was made and agreed upon using the raw commodities themselves. Some forms of plunder, especially rum or other liquor, were   divided at the time of capture, as it would be almost impossible to avoid pilfering during the voyage.

Bartholomew Roberts off the West African coast. In the background a fleet of captured slavers ride at anchor, and guarding them are Roberts' vessels the *Royal Fortune* and the *Great Ranger*. The two flags known to have been flown by the pirate are clearly depicted.

Charter of Bartholomew Roberts' Crew, 1722

Every man shall have an equal vote in affairs of moment. He shall have an equal title to the fresh provisions or strong liquors at any time seized, and shall use them at pleasure unless a scarcity makes it necessary for the common good that a retrenchment may be voted.

Every man shall be called fairly in turn by the list on board of prizes, because over and above their proper share, they are allowed a shift of clothes. But if they defraud the company to the value of even one dollar in plate, jewels or money, they shall be marooned. If any man rob another he shall have his nose and ears slit, and be put ashore where he shall be sure to encounter hardships.

None shall game for money, either with dice or cards.

The lights and candles shall be put out at eight at night, and if any of the crew desire to drink after that hour they shall sit upon the open deck without lights.

Each man shall keep his piece, cutlass and pistols at all times clean and ready for action.

No boy or woman to be allowed amongst them. If any man shall be found seducing one of the latter sex and carrying her to sea in disguise, he shall suffer death.

He that shall desert the ship or his quarters in time of battle shall be punished by death or marooning.

None shall strike another aboard the ship, but every man's quarrel shall be ended on shore by sword or pistol in this manner: at the word of command from the Quartermaster, each man being previously placed back to back, shall turn and fire immediately. If any man do not, the Quartermaster shall knock the piece out of his hand. If both miss their aim, they shall take to their cutlasses, and he that draws first blood shall be declared the victor.

No man shall talk of breaking up their way of living till each has a share of £1,000. Every man who shall become a cripple or lose a limb in the service shall have eight hundred pieces of eight from the common stock, and for lesser hurts proportionately.

The Captain and the Quartermaster shall each receive two shares of a prize, the Master Gunner and Boatswain, one and one half shares, all other officers one and one quarter, and private gentlemen of fortune one share each.

The musicians shall have rest on the Sabbath Day only, by right, on all other days, by favour only.

Many parts of the pirate code were designed to prevent potential sources of conflict among the crew. In fairly strict examples, like those of Roberts' crew, these included rules against gambling, womanising, fighting and drinking, all the elements that are usually associated with pirates. If plundered alcohol was divided, the crew would get drunk, and this inevitably led to conflict. Even Edward Teach recorded problems with keeping the crew happy (and therefore not voting him out of office) when his ship had run out of rum. The codes are an interesting example of man trying to constrain himself against his worst excesses, while being free to indulge in them at will!

PIRATE FLAGS

While the precise origin of the pirate flag remains unknown, its ancestry can be traced with some certainty. They were used to intimidate the enemy or victim, and the flag was designed to conjure up fear and dread. It was an important part of the pirate armoury, and was the pirate's best form of psy-

The pirate Stede Bonnet, shown wearing a wig and armed with a musket. The engraver has incorrectly shown the flag of the pirate Richard Worley instead of Bonnet's. Worley was a small-time pirate killed off Charleston in 1718.

chological warfare, especially when combined with a preceding reputation of not showing any quarter if opposed. If a pirate could intimidate an enemy to heave-to without offering resistance, then danger to the pirate crew would be eliminated, and the victim's ship could be taken undamaged, thus maintaining its value. Threatening images on the flags were often associated with a known pirate (and hence his reputation), or could conjure up more specific warnings. For example, Bartholomew Roberts bore a grudge against the island colonies of Barbados and Martinique, so in their waters he used a flag showing a pirate figure (presumably Roberts himself) standing on two skulls, Under one were the letters 'ABH' (standing for 'A Barbadian's Head'), and under the other was 'AMH' (for 'A Martiniquan's Head'). The threat was clear, and sailors from these colonies would expect no mercy if they offered any resistance.

Identifying an enemy at sea has always been a difficult task. In the 16th century, royal ships painted their sails with national emblems (e.g. Tudor roses for English vessels, Catholic crosses for Spanish ones), but these ships operated in distinctive naval squadrons, treasure '*flotas*' or other armada-like forces. For other vessels, no such symbols were used. Instead, national flags or banners were employed, an identification technique first used in the medieval period. By the 17th and 18th centuries, national symbolism had stabilised enough for publishers to be able to produce flag identification charts, listing the flags of all known maritime nations.

At sea, these symbols indicated national identity, and whether the vessel was potentially friendly or hostile, although this was not always a reliable indication. Privateers or pirates (as well as national warships) often used foreign flags and banners, in order to entice the enemy within range. As long as these flags were replaced with the appropriate national emblem, this was seen as a legitimate *ruse de guerre*. The best policy was usually to assume all shipping was hostile, especially in time of war.

Privateers, approved as such by their national governments, flew their respective national flag (e.g. the cross of St George for England or the Dutch tricolour for Holland. By the mid-17th century, privateers flew privateering symbols in addition to national flags. Without the national flag, they would have been considered as pirates. Although the nature of these early privateering flags is unrecorded, in 1694, an English Admiralty law made the flying of a red privateering symbol mandatory for English privateers. The red flag is depicted in earlier Dutch maritime paintings, but the meaning was not recorded. The red flag today is associated with warning, and in the context of late 17th century privateering, it served the same purpose of warning another vessel not to resist. The flag as defined by the Admiralty in 1694 was an all red flag, known as 'The Red Jack'. Its description as 'that recognised privateering symbol' indicated that the device was flown earlier in the century. Privateers later referred to 'sailing under the Red Jack'. At around the same time a new symbol appeared. References to a black flag were noted in reports of privateering actions, the first in 1697. This was raised by a privateer if the victim's vessel showed any kind of resistance, and was a symbol that little or no quarter would be given. Yellow flags were also mentioned, although unlike their current association with quarantine, their precise meaning in the late 17th century was unknown. Therefore by 1700, red and black were flag colours associated with privateering. When the outlets for legitimate privateering dried up at the end of the War of Spanish Succession in 1714, many privateers turned to piracy. They simply retained their old symbols, although black became the favoured colour. Red continued to be associated with privateering until the 19th century. The American 18th century privateering colour of a red flag overlaid with white horizontal stripes provided the inspiration for part of the existing flag of the USA.

The use of the term 'Jolly Roger' was not a Hollywood myth, and is derived from one of a couple of sources. The French name for the privateering red flag was the *Jolie Rouge* (Jolly Red), and this was said to have been converted into 'Jolly Roger'. Another possible derivation comes from the word 'Roger'. In late 17th century England the word '*rouge*' was used in association with the rouge laws, limiting vagrancy in England. 'Roger' sprang from this, and was used as a slang word for vagabond, beggar or vagrant. The privateering association with 'Sea Beggars' goes back to the phrase used by Dutch privateers (and freedom fighters) in the late 16th century. It continued to be used as a romanticised description of privateers operating in the English Channel, particularly those from the port of Dunkirk. The 'Jolly Roger' described the privateering symbol, whether a red or a black flag. It later changed from the description of a privateering symbol to a piratical one.

The first reference to a modified basic 'Jolly Roger' was in 1700, when the French privateer Emmanuelle Wynne flew a black flag embellished with a skull, crossed bones and an hourglass. It was presumably also used before the turn of the century, although there is no surviving evidence. It may also have indicated that the flyer no longer considered himself a privateer, and was a full-blown pirate. What is known is that following 1700, additional emblems on the basic red or black flags were increasingly associated with piracy, and different symbols were in turn associated with individual pirate captains.

Of these, the most common symbol was the skull, the symbol of death. It was also frequently depicted in association with crossed bones, another death symbol. Both signs were commonly 'momento mori' on 16th and 17th century gravestones all over the British Isles. Other symbols were complete skeletons, spears, swords, hourglasses, initials, hearts, crossed swords, wings and raised glasses. In an era where symbolism in art and everyday life was commonplace, each had a distinct and immediately recognisable meaning. Apart from the death association with bones, skeletons and skulls, dancing skeletons meant dancing a jig with death, a fatalistic reference that meant the flyer didn't care about his fate. This was also the source of the raised glass symbol ('toasting death'). Weapons were a portent of slaughter to come, while hourglasses and wings indicated that time was running out (or flying away). All these symbols can be found in contemporary allegorical paintings of death, or on gravestones.

The symbols were often combined. For instance, Christopher Moody, who operated off the Carolinas in 1717, used a skull and crossbones, a raised sword and a winged hourglass. Edward Teach (Blackbeard) flew a flag depicting a skeleton holding an hourglass and a spear, next to a bleeding heart. In addition to his 'ABH/ AMH' flag, Bartholomew Roberts also flew one depicting a pirate holding an hourglass, alongside a skeleton clutching a spear. The fatalism in pirate symbolism was evident, and it probably applied to pirates as well as their victims.

National flags were still flown, often in an attempt to show that the pirates still wanted to be seen as privateers who only attacked the ships of other nations. If the countries were at peace, or if the pirate held no privateering commission, this meant little or nothing. In 1718 Charles Vane flew the English flag from one mast and a black pirate flag from another. In 1720, Edward England flew a black flag from his mainmast, a red flag from his foremast and the English flag from his ensign staff.

The entrance to Newgate Prison, London. Although most pirates tried in London were held in Marshalsea Prison pending trial, William Kidd was incarcerated in Newgate for a year, a place described by a prisoner as 'an emblem of hell itself'.

NEWGATE.

PIRATE JUSTICE

Most pirates during the golden age knew that their run of luck could not go on for ever. With the odd exception of the pirate who knew when to retire or accept a pardon and start a new life, almost every pirate met death either in battle or on the gallows. If condemned in England, pirates were taken from a prison in London to Execution Dock, at Wapping, on the banks of the River Thames, where a wooden gallows was built on the low-water mark. After a brief prayer from a chaplain, the pirate was allowed a few last words, then he would be hung. After three tides had washed over the body, the corpse was usually buried in an unmarked grave.

From 1701, Admiralty Courts, who oversaw all trials involving crime 'below the high water mark', were established in the American colonies, including English possessions in the Caribbean, and these courts followed the same routines as in England. In the late 17th century, only the captain and leading pirates were hung, but as Admiralty Courts in the Americas

The hanging of a pirate at Execution Dock, Wapping, London. To the left a bailiff carries the silver oar which signified the authority of the Admiralty Court. The spire of St Mary's, Rotherhithe is shown in the background.

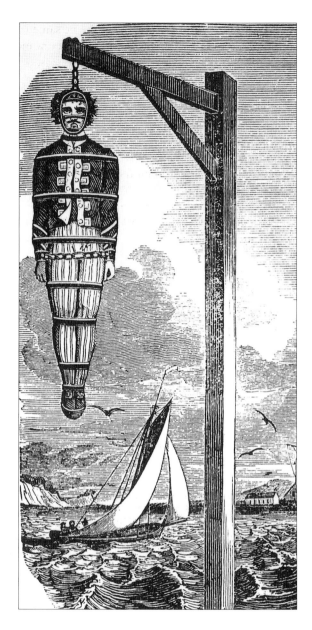

Prominent Admiralty Court executions

May 1701
William Kidd and eight pirates at Execution Dock, London

May 1701
24 French pirates at Execution Dock, London

June 1704
Captain Quelsh and six pirates at Boston, Massachusetts

Summer 1705
Captain Green and 16 pirates on Leith Sands, Edinburgh

November 1716
Jack Rackam and nine pirates in Kingston, Jamaica

October 1717
Seven pirates from Bellamy's crew in Boston, Massachusetts

March 1718
13 pirates from Blackbeard's crew in Williamsburg, Virginia

October 1718
Stede Bonnet and 30 pirates in Charleston, North Carolina

December 1718
Eight pirates captured by Woodes Rogers in New Providence, Bahamas

November 1719
Charles Vane and one pirate in Kingston, Jamaica

March 1722
52 pirates from Roberts' crew in Cape Coast Castle, West Africa

May 1722
Captain Luke and 40 pirates in Kingston, Jamaica

Summer 1723
Captain Finn and four pirates in St. John's, Antigua

July 1723
Captain Harris and 25 pirates in Newport, Rhode Island

March 1724
11 pirates from Captain Lowther's crew in St. Kitts

May 1724
Captain Archer and one pirate in Boston, Massachusetts

May 1725
Captain John Gow and seven pirates at Execution Dock, London

July 1726
Captain William Fly and two pirates in Boston, Massachusetts

July 1727
Captain John Prie at Execution Dock, London

William Kidd's corpse hanging in a cage at Tilbury, on the estuary of the River Thames. For dramatic effect the masthouse at Blackwall is depicted in the background. Corpses were displayed in this gruesome fashion until the body rotted away, a process that could take up to two years. It was designed as a stern warning against sailors tempted to follow in the pirate's footsteps.

cracked down on the pirate scourge during the early years of the 18th century, whole crews were sent to the gallows. This led to a spate of mass trials and hangings, designed to deter others from taking up piracy. In effect, the courts were combating the rise in piratical activities by a propaganda war aimed at potential pirate recruits.

The dates of these executions show that the 'golden age' was really a brief period of ten years, during which the worst pirates and their crews were hunted down, killed in action or executed en masse. The way this business worked is worth examining.

When Captain Ogle captured Bartholomew Roberts' fleet, he netted 264 pirates. This was perhaps the largest pirate band afloat at the time. Of these, 187 were white and 77 were black. Regardless of whether the black prisoners came from West Africa or the Americas, they did not face trial, but instead they were sold into slavery. Captain Ogle, his crew and the admiral of the station shared the profit in the same way they did from the sale of the pirate vessels. The remaining white crew members were brought to trial in Cape Coast Castle. Of these prisoners, 52 were hanged, while 77 were acquitted. Of the remainder, 37 were sent to prison; 20 of these were sentenced to seven years of hard labour in the mines on the African Gold Coast (which was effectively a death sentence), and a further 17 were transported to England where they were imprisoned in Marshalsea Prison for various terms. Two prisoners were released on probation, their sentences frozen 'pending the King's pleasure', they were probably press-ganged into naval service. Nineteen men died of wounds or disease before they could be brought to trial

After a prominent pirate was hanged, the Admiralty Court often wanted to make an example of him, as a warning to others. The body was removed from the gallows and then tied to a post to be washed over three times by the tide, 'as Admiralty law proscribes'. Then the corpse was cut down, tarred, bound in chains and placed inside an iron cage. This was suspended from a gibbet on a prominent headland, often on a busy waterway, or in a similar highly visible location. These gibbets were usually set up at the entrance of ports, like the shore of the Thames Estuary near London, at Gallows Point outside Port Royal, or on Hogg Island, opposite Charleston, North Carolina. The tarred body was left to rot inside its cage, a process that often took up to two years.

This is what happened to the corpse of Captain William Kidd, 'whose body was visible for years after his execution'. The sun, rain and frost rotted the body and seagulls pecked out its eyes, but the cage kept the bones in place, 'as a great terror to all persons from committing ye like crimes'. Pirates later said they would sooner die in battle than 'be hanged up drying, like Kidd'. Due to the cost (and probably the stench), it was usually only the

A captive is subjected to a torture known as 'sweating'. Forced to run around a mast until he dropped, the victim was goaded by the pirates' weapons, and here prodded with a boat-hook and a fork. This early 19th century engraving portrays an incident which reputedly took place in the Caribbean, in 1723.

A pirate being entertained by a
Madagascar woman, in an early 19th
century depiction of life in the island
pirate den. After the East India
Company and the navy made piracy
in the Indian Ocean too risky a venture, many former pirates settled on
the island and took local wives.

pirate captains and sometimes their lieutenants who were displayed in this way after being hanged. Ordinary pirates were simply buried in unmarked graves. Apart from Kidd, Vane, Finn, Archer, Gow, Fly, Prie and Rackam among others had their bodies displayed in this manner.

The rash of pirate trials around the world in the 1720s and the draconian punishments inflicted proved a great deterrent, and directly led to the end of the major piratical activities which plagued European trade.

BIBLIOGRAPHY

General Pirate Histories

All of these are readily available on both sides of the Atlantic, and are recommended reading. The works marked (*) are particularly recommended.

Douglas Botting (ed.), *The Pirates*. Time-Life 'Seafarers' Series (Amsterdam, 1978) *Exceptionally well-illustrated work, but contains many inaccuracies*

David Cordingly and John Falconer, *Pirates Fact and Fiction*. National Maritime Museum, Greenwich (London, 1992) *Short work, emphasising pirate fiction in literature and theatre*

David Cordingly, *Under the Black Flag: Romance and reality of life among the Pirates* (London, 1995) * *Probably the best work on piracy available. A good scholarly study*

David Cordingly (ed.), *Pirates: Terror on the High Seas from the Caribbean to the South China Sea* (Atlanta, 1996) A *superbly illustrated work*

Captain C. Johnson, *A General History of the Robberies and Murders of the Most Notorious Pirates* (Amsterdam, 1724) reprinted numerous times. Last reprinted New Mexico, 1988, *Misleading and inaccurate classic, but the source of most of pirate myth.*

David F. Marley, *Pirates: Adventurers of the High Seas* (London, 1995) * *Well-composed general study, emphasising the buccaneering era*

Marcus Rediker, *Between the Devil and the Deep Blue Sea: Merchant Seamen, Pirates, and the Anglo-American Maritime World, 1700-1750* (Cambridge, 1987) * *Superb and stylish study of maritime history*

Jan Rogozinski, *Pirates! An A-Z Encyclopedia: Brigands, Buccaneers and Privateers in Fact, Fiction and Legend* (New York, 1996) *Contains a full description of every pirate film ever made.*

Other Relevant Works

B.R. Burg, *Sodomy and the Pirate Tradition: English Sea Rovers in the 17th Century Caribbean* (New York, 1983)

Patrick Pringle, *Jolly Roger: The story of the Great Age of Piracy* (London, 1953)

Philip Gosse, *The Pirates' Who's Who: Giving particulars of the lives and deaths of the Pirates and Buccaneers* (New York, 1924, reprinted New Mexico, 1988)

Philip Gosse, *The History of Piracy: Famous Adventures and Daring Deeds of Certain Notorious Freebooters of the Spanish Main* (New York, 1932 reprint ed New Mexico, 1988)

Robert E. Lee, *Blackbeard the Pirate: A reappraisal of his life and times* (North Carolina, 1974)

Jo Stanley (ed.), *Bold in her Breeches* (London, 1995)

A cast-iron 4-pdr. gun, recovered from the English slave ship *Henrietta Marie*, wrecked off Key West, Florida in 1700. It is typical of the size and shape of the ordnance pieces carried on small pirate vessels and merchant ships of the era. The piece carries a weight mark (6-3-24), a proof mark ('P') and an 'S' on the trunnion, indicating that it was made at Stream, East Sussex.

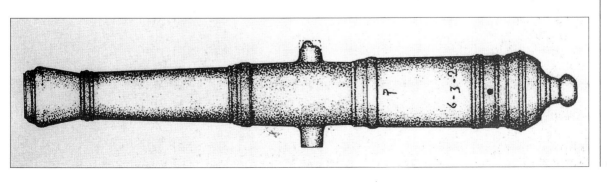

THE PLATES

PLATE A: CAPTAIN KIDD, 1700

William Kidd burying his treasure on Long Island before trying to reach an agreement with the governor of New York, the Earl of Bellamont. The pirate myth of buried treasure has little basis in fact, although Kidd was one of the few who did hide his plunder in this manner. Arrested in Boston soon after the scene depicted here, Kidd was forced by Bellamont to draw up a list of all the plunder he brought back from the Indian Ocean. Convinced that Kidd was hiding some of it, after the plunder caches were dug up, Bellamont and subsequent treasure hunters searched Long Island for years, trying to find more hidden treasure. Writers of pirate fiction such as Robert Louis Stevenson made the burying of treasure an integral part of the piratical image.

Wearing the dress of a gentleman captain as befits his social station, this depiction of Kidd is based upon a contemporary painting, one of the few surviving representations of a pirate. He is armed with a curved smallsword and a large military pistol. His crewmen are dressed in the standard sailor's garb of 'petticoat' breeches and linen shirt. One figure wears a sleeveless vest and the other a silken headscarf.

PLATE B: HENRY EVERY, 1694

Henry Every and the crew of the pirate vessel *Fancy* boarding the treasure ship of the Great Moghul of India, the *Gang-i-sawai*. After gathering a group of fellow pirates together in the Red Sea, Every and his pirate 'fleet' felt strong enough to take on the heavily armed convoy sailing between the Middle East and India. After a night chase, Every's ship found itself within range of the largest ship in the fleet, the *Gang-i-sawai*. What followed was a running gun duel, followed by a vicious boarding action. When the pirates captured the ship, they killed or threw overboard most of their prisoners, raped the women passengers and looted the ship. One of the most successful pirate prizes ever, the captured ship yielded a fortune in gold, silver, jewels, spices, silks and ornaments.

The pirate attackers are depicted wielding a range of weapons, from cutlasses, daggers, axes and pistols to hunting hangers and even an Egyptian-Sudanese short sword. The majority of the crew are shown wearing standard European seaman's clothing, although the black pirate wears an Egyptian form of tunic, and the pirate in the foreground wears a waist sash woven from African cloth.

PLATE C: GOVERNOR ROGERS ENTERING NEW PROVIDENCE, 1718

When Woodes Rogers was appointed governor of the Bahamas, he swore to clear out the nest of pirates based on New Providence Island. Although many of the pirates such as Blackbeard fled before he arrived, and others meekly surrendered, Charles Vane decided to make a statement. Sending a fireship towards the approaching Royal Naval warships carrying the new governor, Vane and his sloop slipped past in the confusion, firing a broadside at the governor's ship in the passing. Although the warships gave chase, Vane eluded them and continued his piratical career.

Governor Rogers is shown dressed in the finery of a gentleman of his station, complete with silk cravat, wig and dress smallsword. Behind him a young naval lieutenant wears a dress uniform jacket thrown over his working dress of a seaman's trousers and linen shirt.

Another 19th century depiction of pirates torturing their captives. It shows an event which took place off the West African coast in 1718, when a prisoner was pelted with broken bottles before being used for target practice.

The head of Edward Teach ('Blackbeard') hanging from the bowsprit of Lieutenant Maynard's sloop, the *Jane,* as it sailed up the James River to anchor in Jamestown Roads, near Williamsburg, Virginia.

PLATE D: GUN AND CREW, EARLY 18TH CENTURY

A cast-iron 8-pdr. gun and crew is shown being prepared for firing. While two pirates haul on the gun tackles to roll the gun and carriage back to the gunport for firing, the gun captain has pricked the touch-hole and is pouring priming powder into the vent. Above them are the principal gun tools: a rammer and ladle combination, a rammer and sponge combination and a worm, used to clean the barrel after firing. While powder was almost exclusively loaded in cartridge form, a ladle was still useful in case of cartridge breakage, or when unloading a gun that failed to fire. A gun of this size could usually be operated by a crew of four, and a well-trained crew could fire and reload in less than two minutes.

Below the gun is an array of ammunition types. From left to right: a roundshot, a flammable spike shot (used to stick in a target and set it on fire), two types of canister shot, a grapeshot sabot, and four variants of anti-rigging projectiles (barshot, splitshot, expanding barshot and chain shot.)

PLATE E: MARY READE AND ANNE BONNY, 1720

Mary Reade and Anne Bonny are depicted rousing 'Calico Jack' Rackam and his drunken crew when the pirates were surprised by a warship off the coast of Jamaica. The two women were unable to pull the men together enough to offer much resistance, and when the ship was boarded, Bonny and Reade were the only crew members who fought their attackers. When they were overpowered the resistance ceased. The captured pirates were taken to Port Royal to stand trial. The women were spared the noose because they were pregnant, but Rackam and the rest of his crew were hanged.

Anne Bonny on the left is dressed in a captured gentleman's waistcoat and breeches, while Mary Reade wears the dress of a common seaman. Bonny is the only armed figure in the scene, carrying a naval service pistol and one of the hunting hangers that were widely used at sea in the early 18th century. The 'onion' bottles carried by Rackam and his fellow reveller are based on examples recovered from the sunken remains of Port Royal, Jamaica. Rackam's feathered hat is based on the Rackam engraving in Johnson's *Pyrates*.

PLATE F: BLACKBEARD'S LAST FIGHT, 1718

Edward Teach (Blackbeard) was tracked down to his lair in Ocracoke Inlet by a naval force of two sloops commanded by Lieutenant Maynard, Royal Navy. One of the sloops was disabled by a broadside from Teach's sloop, and thinking that the second naval vessel was undermanned, Teach came alongside and boarded it. Maynard had hidden most of his crew, who sprang into action, outnumbering the pirates. During the brutal mêlée, Maynard and Teach fought hand-to-hand. The scene depicts the start of the action. Teach and Maynard exchange pistol shots, then draw swords and close for their fight to the death. While the rest of the crews fought around them, the two captains battled alone, until the Highland seaman shown behind Maynard interceded to save his officer. Behind Teach is one of his crewmen, Black Caesar, who tried to end the fight by igniting the pirate vessel's magazine. He was knocked unconscious before he could cause the explosion. After his death, Teach's body was found marked with five bullet wounds and 20 sword cuts.

Teach is depicted in a more realistic manner than the figure portrayed in Johnson's *Pyrates*. The burning slowmatch in his beard is probably an artistic creation, but he did tie his hair with black ribbons, he did have a large black beard and he was a tall, imposing figure. While Maynard wears a naval officer's coat, the remaining crewmen of both sides wear a typical assortment of seamen's garb.

PLATE G: FIREARMS IN THE EARLY 18TH CENTURY

The central figure is shown ready to fire a 1-pdr. swivel gun, which is typical of the rail guns carried on pirate vessels, privateers and warships during the early 18th century. It fired a cluster of musket balls into the faces of the enemy to clear the decks before boarding. At the top of the picture a short-barrelled blunderbuss is shown above a military grenade launcher converted to project a grappling hook. These weapons were occasionally used on privateers and warships. A soldier's cartridge block represents the style of the box worn by Blackbeard which blocked Lieutenant Maynard's sword thrust. A shot mould is overlaid on an English military musket of 1700. Next to it is the equivalent French weapon.

At the bottom left is a musketoon, a form of short-calibre blunderbuss that was more accurate than a blunderbuss at anything other than point-blank range. A large sea service pistol of the type recovered from the wreck of the pirate ship *Whydah* (1717) is shown above the smaller Queen Anne pistol which was favoured because of its compact size.

PLATE H: STEDE BONNET'S EXECUTION, 1718

The 'gentleman pirate' had a short and ignominious career spanning 20 months in 1717 and 1718. He started by abandoning his plantation holdings in Barbados, buying a sloop, hiring a crew and setting off to sea as a pirate: a unique way for a landsman to start a pirate career. After being captured by Edward Teach for several months, he was released, pardoned by a colonial governor, and promptly returned to piracy. After being caught he was brought to Charleston to face trial and execution. As a former gentleman he expected a degree of leniency, but instead the judge used the trial as an opportunity to moralise on social issues, and he was sentenced to death. It was reported that, 'His piteous behaviour under sentence very much affected the people of the Province, particularly the women.' His pleas for clemency from the governor of South

Carolina were ignored, and Bonnet was hanged along with 30 of his crew.

The scene depicts the mechanics of a pirate execution. Hanged below the high-water mark of the harbour to emphasise the authority of the Admiralty Court, the pirate's body was then cut down and chained to a post between high and low-water mark. Once the tide had ebbed and flowed over the body three times (i.e. 36 hours later) the body was removed. Common pirates were buried in unmarked graves, but the bodies of pirate captains were frequently tarred, bound inside an iron cage and suspended from a gibbet overlooking a busy waterway. The body would remain as a warning against piracy until the corpse completely rotted away.

PLATE I: BARTHOLOMEW ROBERTS, 1723

Bartholomew Roberts during his final moments, just before he was killed by the broadside from HMS *Swallow*. One of the most colourful and successful pirates of the era, the Welsh-born Roberts cut a swathe through the Caribbean, the colonial American seaboard and West Africa for 30 months. During his career he captured a record 200 ships,

and changed his flagship for consistently bigger and better ships. He bore a grudge against the inhabitants of Martinique and Barbados, and even managed to capture the French governor of Martinique and hang him from his own ship's yardarm. In his final battle, Roberts' ship the *Royal Fortune* was surprised by the frigate HMS *Swallow*, commanded by Captain Ogle, Royal Navy. The pirate crew had been revelling after capturing a prize the day before, and they were therefore not at their peak when the battle started. Killed in the first broadside while standing on a gun, Roberts died of a gaping wound to the throat. His crew pitched his body overboard to prevent it being captured, and then fought on for another couple of hours before being overwhelmed and captured.

Roberts is depicted according to the account by Johnson, which describes him 'dressed in a rich crimson damask waistcoat and breeches, a red feather in his hat, a gold chain round his neck, with a diamond cross hanging to it'. The faces of the men behind him reflect the multi-racial mix of Roberts' crew. Behind him flies one of Roberts' flags, showing the pirate drinking a toast with death.

PLATE J: EDGED WEAPONS IN THE EARLY 18TH CENTURY

The pirate in the centre armed with a cutlass is shown wearing a seaman's jacket, 'petticoat breeches', a crimson silk waist sash and a woollen cap. All but the waist sash were typical of sailors' dress during the early 18th century.

Top left: a cutlass, next to a hunting hanger and a converted amalgam between the two forms of weapons.

Top right: two forms of military or naval swords, a cavalry broadsword and an officer's smallsword.

Right: a boarding pike with langets to prevent the head being chopped off, and a boarding axe.

Below these are examples of daggers. The first is a standard dagger as carried by seamen in the period, and below it, a converted plug bayonet. These found their way onto privateers at the end of the War of Spanish Succession, and were converted to be used to cut as well as thrust. Behind it is a boathook, indicative of the fact that scattered throughout sailing ships re many forms of improvised weaponry, axes, hooks, belaying pins and gun tools. Bottom right is a late 17th

Edward England, wearing a gentleman's coat and smallsword with the battle between his ship the *Fancy* and the East Indiaman *Cassandra* depicted in the background. After a brutal action where the two ships cannoned each other for hours, the *Cassandra* surrendered. England's leniency towards the enemy crew led to his removal as captain.

century military basket-hilted sword, of the type that was probably used to kill 'Blackbeard' in 1718.

PLATE K: PIRATE FLAGS

Top Row, left: Edward Teach (Blackbeard); right: Stede Bonnet. Variants of the skeleton theme, the hearts represent danger, and the weapons violence.

Second Row, left: 'Calico' Jack Rackam; right: Edward Low. Similar designs to those above, the Rackam flag is a novel variant of the classic pirate emblem.

Third Row, Christopher Moody. A colourful flag, it manages to contain most of the popular symbolism into one design; time flying away, threat of a violent end and imminent death

Fourth Row, left: Henry Every; right: Bartholomew Roberts. Every's variation on the standard skull and crossbones was displayed on both black and red fields. Of the two known Bartholomew Roberts flags, his drinking with death emblem turned out to be most appropriate. When his ship was attacked and Roberts killed, most of the crew had been drinking well into the previous night.

Fifth Row, left: Bartholomew Roberts; right: Edward England. Roberts' flag indicates the strength of his hatred for the inhabitants of the   island colonies of Barbados and Martinique by picturing a pirate (presumably Roberts himself) astride two skulls labelled ABH and AMH. The letters stand for 'A Barbadian's Head' and 'A Martiniquan's Head'. England's flag became famous when it was adopted by later writers of pirate fiction, including Robert Louis Stevenson. It is now considered the archetypal pirate flag, although, as can be seen here, the range of flags used was actually much greater.

In this early 19th century engraving, pirates are shown whipping and humiliating a pair of Portuguese priests, captured off the Brazilian coast in 1718 by an unidentified pirate crew. Religious differences often resulted in the torture and death of Catholic priests or officials captured by pirates.

Notes sur les Planches en Couleur

A: Le Capitaine Kidd, 1700 William Kidd en train d'enterrer son trésor sur Lond Island.
Il porte l'uniforme d'un gentleman-capitaine, comme il se doit pour son rang, et il est armé d'un glaive recourbé et d'un gros pistolet militaire. Les hommes de son équipage portent l'habit standard des marins: un pantalon bouffant et une chemise de lin. L'un des personnages porte un gilet sans manches et l'autre un foulard de soie.

B: Henry Every, 1694 Henry Every et l'équipage du vaisseau pirate Fancy en train d'aborder le bateau du Grand Mogul d'Inde, le Gang-i-sawai, chargé de matières précieuses. Les pirates brandissent des armes diverses: coutelas, poignards, haches et pistolets, poignards de chasse et même une épée égypto-soudanaise. La plupart d'entre eux porte la tenue standard des marins européens, mais le pirate noir porte une forme de tunique égyptienne et le pirate au premier plan porte une ceinture en tissu africain.

C: Le gouverneur Rogers arrivant à New Providence, 1718 Le Gouverneur Rogers est représenté portant les beaux atours d'un gentilhomme de son rang, avec foulard-cravate de soie, perruque et glaive. Derrière lui, un jeune lieutenant de marine porte une veste de grande tenue par-dessus son uniforme de travail, composé du pantalon et de la chemise de lin des marins.

D: Pièce et équipe, début du XVIIIe On prépare un canon en fonte de 8 livres au tir. Au-dessus, les outils principaux: un refouloir et poche, un refouloir et éponge et un tire-bourre, utilisé pour nettoyer le baril après le tir. En-dessous, une gamme de munitions. De gauche à droite: un boulet rond, une pointe incendiaire, deux types de mitraille, un sabot à mitraille et quatre projectiles anti-gréements: une barre, une barre à mitraille, une barre extensible et une chaîne.

E: Mary Reade et Anne Bonny, 1720 Mary Reade et Anne Bonny sont représentées en train de réveiller "Calico Jack" Rackam et son équipage ivre lorsque les pirates furent surpris par un navire de guerre au large des côtes de la Jamaïque. Anne Bonny, sur la gauche, porte le gilet et la culotte d'un gentilhomme capturé, alors que Mary Reade porte les vêtements d'un marin commun. Bonny est le seul personnage armé de la scène: elle porte un pistolet de service naval et l'un des poignards de chasse communément utilisés.

F: Le dernier combat de Barbe-noire, 1718 Edward Teach (Barbe-noire) fut traqué et tué par une force navale commandée par le Lieutenant Maynard, de la Royal Navy. Teach attachait effectivement ses cheveux avec des rubans noirs, il avait une grande barbe noire et c'était un homme grand et imposant. Maynard porte le manteau d'un officier naval.

G: Les armes à feu au début du XVIIIe Le personnage central est illustré prêt à mettre un canon à pivot de 1,5 livre à feu. En haut, un tromblon à baril court est illustré au-dessus d'un lanceur de grappins. Un moule à boulet est placé sur un mousquet militaire anglais. A côté, l'arme française équivalente. En bas à gauche, un mousqueton, sorte de tromblon à canon court. Un grand pistolet de service maritime est illustré au-dessus du type Reine Anne plus compact.

H: Exécution de Stede Bonnet, 1718 Ce "gentleman-pirate" eut une carrière courte et ignominieuse. Il a été pendu au-dessous de la ligne de la marée haute dans le port pour souligner l'autorité du Tribunal de l'Amirauté. Le corps du pirate fut ensuite enchaîné à un poteau entre les deux marées. Lorsque la marée eut descendu et remonté sur le corps trois fois, il fut détaché. Les pirates communs étaient enterrés dans des fosses communes, mais le corps des capitaines pirates était souvent plongé dans du goudron et placé dans une cage en fer au-dessus d'une voie d'eau fréquentée en guise d'avertissement contre la piraterie.

I: Bartholomew Roberts, 1723 Bartholomew Roberts dans ses derniers moments, juste avant d'être tué par une bordée du HMS Swallow. Roberts est représenté selon la description de Johnson: "portant un gilet et une culotte de riche damas cramoisi, avec une plume rouge au chapeau, une chaîne d'or autour du cou, d'où pendait une croix de diamant" Le visage des hommes derrière lui reflète le mélange de races dans l'équipage de Roberts.

J: Armes tranchantes du début du XVIIIe Le pirate au centre, armé d'un coutelas porte une veste de marin, un pantalon large, une ceinture en soie cramoisie et un calot en laine. Tous ces éléments, à part la ceinture, sont typiques de l'habillement des marins au début du XVIIIe. En haut à gauche: un coutelas, à côté d'un poignard de chasse et un amalgame des deux formes d'armes. En haut à droite: un sabre de cavalerie et un glaive d'officier. A droite: une pique d'abordage et une hache d'abordage. En dessous, divers exemples de poignards. Le premier est un poignard standard et, en-dessous, une baïonnette modifiée. Derrière, une gaffe. En bas à droite, une épée à garde en vannerie de la fin du XVIIe siècle.

K: Drapeaux de pirates Rang supérieur: Edward Teach (Barbe-noire); à droite: Stede Bonnet. Des variations sur le thème du squelette. Les coeurs représentent le danger, et les armes la violence. Second rang, à gauche;"Calico" Jack Rackam; à droite: Edward Low. Troisième rang: Christopher Moody. Contient la plupart des symbolismes populaires: le temps qui s'enfuit, la menace d'une mort violente et une mort imminente. Quatrième rang: à gauche: Henry Every; à droite: Bartholomew Roberts. La variation d'Every sur la tête de mort standard était présentée sur fond noir et sur fond rouge. Cinquième rang à gauche: Bartholomew Roberts; droite: Edward England. Le drapeau de Roberts indique l'intensité de sa haine pour les habitants des îles colonies de La Barbade et de la Martinique. Le drapeau d'Edward England est aujourd'hui considéré comme le drapeau pirate type.

Farbtafeln

A: Captain Kidd, 1700: William Kidd beim Vergraben seines Schatzes auf Long Island. Er trägt die Kapitänskleidung eines Gentlemans, wie es seiner gesellschaftlichen Stellung geziemt. Er ist mit einem kurzen Krummsäbel und einer großen Militärpistole bewaffnet. Seine Männer tragen die damals übliche Matrosenkleidung, die aus „Petticoat-Breeches" und einem Leinenhemd bestand. Ein Matrose trägt ein ärmelloses Unterhemd, ein anderer ein Seidenkopftuch.

B: Henry Every, 1694: Henry Every und die Mannschaft des Piratenschiffes Fancy gehen an Bord der Gang-i-sawai, das mit Schätzen beladene Schiff des Großmoguls von Indien. Beim Angriff schwingen die Piraten eine breit gefächerte Palette von Waffen, darunter Entermesser, Dolche, Äxte und Pistolen sowie Weidmesser und sogar ein ägyptisch-sudanesisches Kurzschwert. Der Großteil der Mannschaft ist in der üblichen europäischen Seemannskleidung abgebildet, obwohl der schwarze Pirat eine Art ägyptische Tunika und der Pirat im Vordergrund eine Schärpe aus afrikanischem Tuch trägt.

C: Gouverneur Rogers bei der Ankunft in New Providence, 1718: Gouverneur Rogers trägt die prächtige Kleidung, eines Gentleman seiner Stellung zukommt, sowie eine Seidenkrawatte und eine Perücke, und er hat einen Paradesäbel bei sich. Hinter ihm sieht man einen Kapitänleutnant, der die Jacke seiner Ausgeuniform über den aus Seemannshosen und Leinenhemd bestehenden Arbeitsanzug geworfen hat.

D: Geschütz und Mannschaft, Anfang des 18. Jahrhunderts: Ein gußeisernes 8-pdr-Geschütz wird zum Feuern bereit gemacht. Darüber sieht man die wichtigsten Geschützwerkzeuge: eine Ansetzer-Kelle-Kombination, eine Ansetzer-Schwamm-Kombination und die Schneckengewinde, mit dem der Geschützlauf nach dem Feuern gereinigt wird. Darunter sind die verschiedenen Munitionsarten abgebildet. Von links nach rechts: ein Rundgeschoß, ein brennbares Stachelgeschoß, zwei Arten von Kartätschen, ein Kartätschengeschoßring und vier Takelwerkverteidigungsgeschosse - Stangenkugel, Spaltgeschoß, expandierende Stangenkugel und Kettengeschoß.

E: Mary Reade und Anne Bonny, 1720: Mary Reade und Anne Bonny sind auf diesem Bild gerade dabei, 'Calico' Jack Rackam und seine betrunkene Mannschaft wachzurütteln. Die Piraten waren von einem Kriegsschiff vor der Küste von Jamaika überrascht worden. Anne Bonny auf der linken Seite trägt die von den Piraten ergatterte Weste und Breeches eines Gentlemans, während Mary Reade die Kleidung eines gewöhnlichen Matrosen trägt. Bonny ist als einzige bewaffnet und hat eine Marinepistole und eines der weitverbreiteten Weidmesser bei sich.

F: Blackbeards letzter Kampf, 1718: Edward Teach (Blackbeard) wurde von Marinetruppen unter dem Kommando von Kapitänleutnant Maynard, Royal Navy, aufgespürt und getötet. Teach hielt sein Haar tatsächlich mit schwarzen Bändern zusammen und hatte wirklich einen buschigen schwarzen Bart. Er war von großer, imposanter Gestalt. Maynard trägt den Rock eines Marineoffiziers.

G: Schußwaffen am Anfang des 18. Jahrhunderts: Die in der Mitte abgebildete Figur ist bereit, ein 11/2-pdr-Drehgeschütz abzufeuern. Oben ist eine Donnerbüchse mit kurzem Lauf abgebildet, darunter eine Enterhaken-Abschußvorrichtung. Über einer englischen Militärmuskete sieht man eine Geschoßgußform. Daneben ist das französische Geschütz gezeigt. Unten links sieht man ein sogenanntes „Musketoon", eine Art kleinkalibriger Donnerbüchse. Eine große Pistole für den Dienst zur See ist über dem kompakteren Queen Anne-Modell abgebildet.

H: Die Hinrichtung von Stede Bonnet, 1718: Der „Gentleman-Pirat" hatte eine kurze, unehrenhafte Laufbahn. Er wurde unterhalb des Hochwasserstandzeichens des Hafens aufgehängt, um die Amtsgewalt des Marinegerichts zu betonen. Anschließend wurde die Leiche des Piraten an einen Pfosten zwischen der Hoch- und Niedrigwassermarke gekettet. Wenn Ebbe und Flut drei Mal über die Leiche gespült hatten, wurde sie abgenommen. Gewöhnliche Piraten wurden in nicht gekennzeichneten Gräbern beerdigt, aber die Leichen von Piratenkapitänen wurden häufig geteert und in einem Eisenkäfig an einer viel befahrenen Wasserstraße zur Abschreckung zur Schau gestellt.

I: Bartholomew Roberts, 1723: Bartholomew Roberts in den letzten Augenblicken seines Lebens, unmittelbar bevor er von einer Breitseite der HMS Swallow getötet wurde. Die Darstellung von Roberts beruht auf dem Bericht von Johnson, der ihn folgendermaßen beschrieb: „Er trug eine satt karmesinrote Damaskweste und Breeches, hatte eine rote Feder am Hut und eine Goldkette um den Hals, an der ein Diamantkreuz hing." Die Gesichter der Männer hinter ihm spiegeln die vielen verschiedenen Rassen, aus denen sich Roberts' Mannschaft zusammensetzte.

J: Klingenwaffen Anfang des 18. Jahrhunderts: Der Pirat in der Mitte ist mit einem kurzen Säbel bewaffnet und trägt eine Seemannsjacke, „Petticoat-Breeches", eine karmesinrote Seidenschärpe und eine Wollmütze. Abgesehen von der Schärpe sind die Kleidungsstücke für die Matrosenkleidung Anfang des 18. Jahrhunderts typisch. Oben links: ein kurzer Säbel, daneben ein Weidmesser und eine umgerüstete Mischung aus den beiden Arten von Waffe. Oben rechts: ein Kavallerie-Pallasch und ein Offiziersdegen. Rechts: ein Enterhaken und eine Enteraxt. Darunter sind verschiedene Dolche abgebildet. Beim ersten handelt es sich um einen Standarddolch, darunter ist ein umgerüstetes Pfropfenbajonett. Dahinter sieht man einen Bootshaken. Unten rechts ist ein Militärschwert mit Korbgeflechtheft aus dem späten 17. Jahrhundert abgebildet.

K: Piratenflaggen: Oberste Reihe: - links: Edward Teach (Blackbeard); **rechts:** Stede Bonnet. Verschiedene Ausführungen des Skelett-Motivs, die Herzen versinnbildlichen Gefahr, die Waffen Gewalt. **Zweite Reihe - links:** 'Calico' Jack Rackam; **rechts:** Edward Low. **Dritte Reihe:** Christopher Moody. Die meisten der populären Symbole sind vertreten: der schnelle Lauf der Zeit, die Gefahr eines gewalttätigen Endes und der kurz bevorstehende Tod. **Vierte Reihe - links:** Henry Every; **rechts:** Bartholomew Roberts. Everys Variante des üblichen Symbols mit Totenkopf und gekreuzten Knochen erschien sowohl auf schwarzem als auch rotem Hintergrund. **Fünfte Reihe - links:** Bartholomew Roberts; **rechts:** Edward England. Roberts' Flagge beweist, wie sehr er die Bewohner der Inselkolonien Barbados und Martinique haßte. Edward Englands Flagge gilt inzwischen als die archetypische Piratenflagge.